Kids Write Right!

What You Need to Be a **Writing Powerhouse**

●●●●●●●●●●●●●●●●●●●●●●●●●●

Jan Venolia

Tricycle Press
Berkeley • Toronto

Hi!

I hope you enjoy using *Kids Write Right!* and that it helps with your schoolwork. I've packed in a lot of information and made it easy to understand.

Do you have ideas about something you think I should include in future editions? What do you like about the book or wish were different? Do you think a *Kids Write Right!* workbook is a good idea?

I'd like to hear from you. Good luck!

Jan Venolia
c/o Tricycle Press
P.O. Box 7123
Berkeley, CA 94707

Tricycle Press
P.O. Box 7123
Berkeley, California 94707
www.tenspeed.com

The typographic scheme and jacket design are by Jeff Puda.
The text of this book was set in Tarzana Narrow, Granjon, & Gothic 821.

Library of Congress Cataloging-in-Publication Data
Venolia, Jan.
Kids write right! : what you need to be a writing powerhouse / by Jan Venolia.
p. cm.   Includes index.
ISBN 1-58246-028-0 (pbk.)
1. English language—Study and teaching (Middle school)—Juvenile literature. 2. English language—Grammar—Study and teaching (Middle school)—Juvenile literature. [1. English language—Grammar. 2. Authorship. 3. Writing.] I. Title.
LB1631.V45 2000   428.2—dc21   00-030272

First printing, 2000
Printed in Canada
1 2 3 4 5 6 — 04 03 02 01 00

Contents

1

Why Should I Care about Good Writing?

●●●●●●●●●●●●●●●●●●●●●●●●●●●●

Does Good Writing Matter?

Good question. Why not just throw words on paper and let people figure them out? Because good writing helps people understand what you want to say. In other words, it helps you communicate.

Communication helps all of us on this planet get to know each other, and writing is one of the important ways we communicate. Even e-mail is writing, after all, so it helps if you do it well. People shouldn't have to struggle to understand what you've written. You want them to follow your line of thought, so don't wander off, jumping from subject to subject. Your readers might wander off, too!

In the process of writing, you learn about your subject. And the more you learn, the more interesting life becomes.

Learning to write is a good survival skill. It could help you get a job someday. Students have the idea that once they graduate, they won't have to write. But writing is important in many jobs, and knowing how to do it well gives you an edge over the competition. Now, when you're young, is the best time to learn.

Writing is a handy tool. Here are just a few ways you can use it.

- ✓ To enter contests

- ✓ To get information

- ✓ To get free stuff

- ✓ To complain about something you bought that doesn't work

- ✓ To get good grades

- ✓ To thank someone

- ✓ To convince someone of something important

Let's look at the last item on the list. Students in Anoka, Minnesota, used writing as part of their campaign to convince the city council to redesign and modernize the city park. They also used it to save and restore a historic amphitheater for concerts and plays. Once the students saw what they could accomplish, they kept it up. They've been improving their community for years now. (You can read more about their story on page 127.)

Good writing *does* get results. It opens doors and makes interesting things happen.

What Is Good Writing?

It is

- ✓ Clear (You don't confuse anyone.)

- ✓ Concise (You use just enough words to make your point.)

- ✓ Correct (You use the right grammar, punctuation, and spelling.)

- ✓ Bias-free (You don't offend readers with words that belittle them.)

- ✓ Well organized (You don't yank readers around.)

- ✓ Interesting (You have something to say.)

How Will *Kids Write Right!* Help Me Write Better?

First, I'll equip you with some handy tools: definitions and rules of grammar.

"Yikes! I hate definitions," I hear you saying. "I hate grammar."

Relax. I'm going to take a tough subject and make it easy. I limit definitions to the "bare necessities," but some terms will help us slay the grammar dragon. In fact, when you see that "What You Need to Know about Grammar" is just half a dozen rules, I think you'll agree that it's more like a pet iguana than a dragon.

I aim to make the other subjects as easy to understand as possible, too: punctuation, spelling and capitalization, tricky words, organization, and writing style. If you find any terms you don't know, you can look them up in the glossary. And the index in the back of the book lists everything covered in *Kids Write Right!*

I've highlighted parts of the book so that you'll know what to expect. Look for these icons.

 Cross-Reference (if you want more information)

 Remember? (when I repeat something as a reminder)

 Important! (when I want you to pay special attention)

Bonus (if you want to tackle the harder parts)

Kids Write Right! answers questions that come up when you're working on an assignment: Does a comma go here? What's a *predicate*? Should I use *who* or *whom*?

Kids Write Right! is a companion for your textbook. It boils the rules down to make them easier to understand and illustrates them with examples.

That's important! **Be sure to look at the examples.** They are often the best way to figure out what a rule is all about.

And remember, the more you practice writing, the better you become at it and the easier it becomes.

● ●

Writing is easy. All you have to do is cross out the wrong words.

—Mark Twain

2

Bringing Grammatical Definitions Down to Earth

● ●

Parts of Speech

Writing begins with words. We put words into sentences and sentences into paragraphs.

Each word in a sentence has a job. Some words describe, some connect, some provide action. We call these jobs **parts of speech**.

There are eight parts of speech.

- ✓ Noun
- ✓ Verb
- ✓ Pronoun
- ✓ Adjective
- ✓ Adverb
- ✓ Preposition
- ✓ Conjunction
- ✓ Interjection

Let's look at each of the parts of speech and what they do. We'll start with nouns and verbs because they are so important.

Nouns name things.

- ✓ **Things you can touch**
    earphones   carrot   backpack   book
- ✓ **Places**
    home base   museum   mall   virtual reality   black hole
- ✓ **Emotions**
    panic   excitement   anger   love   curiosity
- ✓ **Acts**
    inquiry   defiance   agreement   refusal
- ✓ **Ideas**
    freedom   justice   power   forgiveness   honor
- ✓ **Qualities**
    color   beauty   bravery   flexibility   humor   mystery

✓ **People**

gymnast   pianist   doctor   uncle   brat   bully

✓ **Times**

noon   midnight   spring   season   recess   vacation

✓ **Animals**

penguin   boa constrictor   **aardvark**

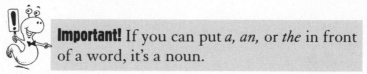

You'll be seeing a lot more of me!

And many more! There are more nouns than any other part of speech in the English language .

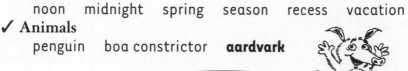

Important! If you can put *a, an,* or *the* in front of a word, it's a noun.

We call the ordinary kind of noun, like those above, **common nouns**. The name we give to a *particular* thing, place, or person is **proper noun**.

Common Noun	Proper Noun
planet	Mars
woman	Amelia Earhart
team	Dallas Cowboys
character	Charlie Brown
monument	Eiffel Tower
relative	Uncle Joe
country	Canada
mountain	Mt. Everest

We capitalize proper nouns to make them stand out from common nouns.

Verbs provide the action; they tell what's happening. A sentence isn't complete without a verb.

> I **fly** my kite.

Verbs also describe a "state of being." This kind of verb is called a **linking verb**.

> I **am** a kite-flying demon.
> Pandas **exist** in just a few places.

When you're feeling a certain way, you can describe it with a linking verb.

> I **feel** tired after running a mile in P.E.

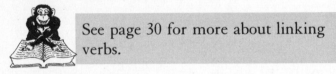

See page 30 for more about linking verbs.

Some verbs need an **object** to complete their meaning.

> Carol **bought** the **book**.
>   verb   object

Without the object, we don't know what Carol bought.

There are two kinds of objects: **direct** and **indirect**.

> **Direct Object:** Riley **found** an **earring**.
>   verb   direct object

The direct object *earring* tells us *what* Riley found.

> **Indirect Object:** Riley **gave** **Allegra** the **earring**.
>   verb indirect object   direct object

The indirect object *Allegra* receives the direct object; the indirect object tells us *who* received the earring.

Verbs that *take an object* are called **transitive**.

> She **hit** the ball.

Ball is the object of the verb *hit. Hit* is a transitive verb.

Verbs that *do not take an object* are called **intransitive**.

> They **laughed** when she hit the ball.

Laughed does not have an object. It's an intransitive verb. *Hit* does have an object: *ball*. It's a transitive verb.

See page 23 for more about verbs.

Pronouns are handy substitutes for nouns; they save you from having to repeat words. This is particularly convenient if what the pronoun is replacing is long or complicated.

> The adolescent African aardvark was lost in the storm.
> **It** was later found vacationing in Hawaii.
> pronoun

That's my name. Don't wear it out!

You can see that if you have much to say about the aardvark, repeating its whole name would be awkward! However, when you replace words with a pronoun, make sure the reader can tell what it has replaced.

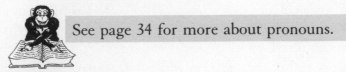

See page 34 for more about pronouns.

Adjectives

Adjectives describe nouns and pronouns. A fancy word that means the same thing as describe is *modify*. Grammarians love fancy words. All you need to remember about this one is that when one word modifies another word, it tells more about it. I'll be using this word a lot!

Here are some adjectives that are modifying nouns.

colorful dragon kite   **peanut butter** cookies
baseball card collection   **acoustic** guitar

If you dress up the word *kite* with adjectives (*colorful* and *dragon*), you create a better picture of the kite. *Acoustic* modifies *guitar*, describing what type of guitar, and *peanut butter* modifies *cookies*.

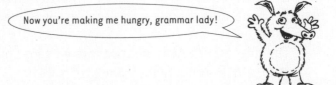

Now you're making me hungry, grammar lady!

Adjectives also tell *how many* there are (*three* peanut butter cookies) and *which* ones they are (*those* peanut butter cookies).

The words *a, an,* and *the* are a special kind of adjective; we call them **articles**. They tell you that a noun is coming. It may not be the very next word, but it will show up soon.

a kite   **the** sturdy centipede-shaped **kite**
article noun   article   noun

Adverbs modify verbs, adjectives, or other adverbs. (There's that word *modify* again!) It means that an adverb tells more about a verb, adjective, or other adverb.

Adverbs can be tricky, since they show up in so many different places in a sentence. But don't worry. Go get some brain food (bananas are good); then come back and read the rest of this section. You can do it!

So, off we go. Here's an adverb modifying a verb.

I **play** computer games **obsessively**.
   verb   adverb

In this sentence, the adverb *obsessively* modifies the verb *play;* it tells *how* I play computer games.

Here's an adverb modifying an adjective.

I play **extremely difficult** computer games.
       adverb   adjective

The adverb *extremely* tells *how* difficult the computer games are: not just a little difficult, *extremely* difficult.

The two adverbs in the sentence below have different jobs: One modifies another adverb, and the other modifies a verb.

I **win** computer games **very often**.
 verb   adverb adverb

The adverb *very* modifies the adverb *often* (how often? *very* often), and the adverb *often* modifies the verb *win* (when do I win computer games? *often*).

All three jobs of the adverb (modifying a verb, an adjective, and an adverb) are in the following sentence. Can you find them?

I win extremely complicated computer games very often.

Answer: The adverb *extremely* modifies the adjective *complicated;* the adverb *very* modifies the adverb *often;* the adverb *often* modifies the verb *win.*

Prepositions connect nouns and pronouns to the rest of the sentence.

The story was written **by** Bruce Coville.

I'm learning to snowboard **with** Midori.

This secret is just **between** you and me.

In Australia, you can order pizza **with** kangaroo medallions and emu sausage.

SUDDENLY I DON'T FEEL LIKE PIZZA ANYMORE

What the preposition connects to the rest of the sentence is called its **object**.

They poked pins **into** their **balloons**.
                preposition   object of preposition

The noise **of** the popping **balloons** hurt my ears.
        preposition   object of preposition

Some prepositions show direction.

I flew my kite **into** a tree.

Some prepositions show time.

I flew my kite **after** the storm.
I flew my kite **during** the storm.

Some prepositions show location.

I flew my kite **over** the roof.
I hid my kite **under** the bed.

The nine most common prepositions are *at, by, for, from, in, of, on, to,* and *with*.

Conjunctions are different kinds of connectors. They hook together individual words.

I like kites **and** rollerblades.
conjunction

They also connect groups of words (clauses).

I fly kites, **but** I also play soccer.
clause   conjunction   clause

There's more to know about clauses. If you just can't wait to find out what it is, turn to page 41 and read The Building Blocks of Sentences. But here, where our topic is conjunctions, it's probably enough to know that clauses are groups of words, and that some are complete thoughts while others are incomplete.

We use different words to describe the three functions of conjunctions.

She's a poet!

Coordinating conjunctions connect terms that are grammatically equal: nouns, verbs, phrases, and clauses.

Connecting Nouns: pizzas **and** roller coasters
red, white, **and** blue
this, **but** not that
Pauline **or** Paul

Connecting Verbs: sneezing **and** coughing
sink **or** swim

Connecting Phrases:

> surfing the net, singing in the rain, **and** whistling in the dark

Connecting Clauses:

> I build kites, **but** I also repair spaceships.

The clauses must each be complete sentences.

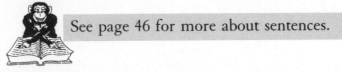

See page 46 for more about sentences.

Common coordinating conjunctions are *and, but, or, nor, for, so, yet.*

Subordinating conjunctions connect clauses that are *not* equally important.

> I play computer games **while** taking care of my little brother.
> independent clause   subordinating   dependent clause
>   conjunction

"I play computer games" is the main clause; it could stand by itself as a complete sentence. "Taking care of my little brother" depends on the main clause to make sense; we use a subordinating conjunction (*while*) to hook it to the main clause.

Common subordinating conjunctions are *after, although, as, as if, as long as, because, though, unless, until, when, while.*

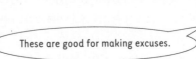
These are good for making excuses.

Correlative conjunctions come in pairs, separated by other words. Examples: *either . . . or, neither . . . nor, not only . . . but also, both . . . and, whether . . . or.*

> **Both** bungee jumping **and** paragliding take you to high places.
> correlative conjunction   correlative conjunction

Interjections are exclamations! When you put strong feelings into just one word, you use an interjection.

Wow!   Oops!   Yikes!   Cool!   Rats!   Ouch!

Interjections give us a chance to use exclamation points.

● ●

Important! The same word can be a noun in one sentence and a verb in another. Or a word that's an adjective in one sentence is a noun in another.

I **fly** my kite.   The **fly** landed on the wall.
  verb   noun

He read the **book**.   He joined a **book** club.
       noun   adjective

Until you see how a word is used in a sentence, you may not be able to tell which part of speech it is.

Parts of Speech Review

Take the basic sentence...

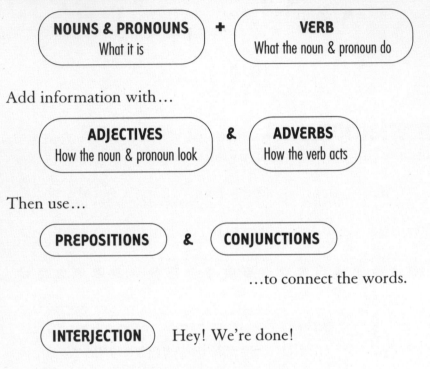

NOUNS & PRONOUNS
What it is

+

VERB
What the noun & pronoun do

Add information with...

ADJECTIVES
How the noun & pronoun look

&

ADVERBS
How the verb acts

Then use...

PREPOSITIONS

&

CONJUNCTIONS

...to connect the words.

INTERJECTION   Hey! We're done!

Grab some nouns...   **aardvark   creek**
  and verbs.   **jumped   thought   am doing**

Add adjectives...   **the   able   roaring**
  and an adverb.   **really**

Pick up some pronouns... **he   I   it**
  and a preposition.   **over**

Catch a conjunction...   **as**
  and insist on
  an interjection!   **Cool!**

Put them all together.

<u>As</u> <u>the</u> <u>able</u> <u>aardvark</u> <u>jumped</u> <u>over</u> <u>the</u> <u>roaring</u> <u>creek</u>, <u>he</u>
conj. adj. adj.   noun   verb   prep. adj.   adj.   noun   pron.

<u>thought</u>, "<u>Cool!</u> <u>I</u> <u>really</u> <u>am doing</u> <u>it</u>."
  verb   interj. pron. adv.   verb   pron.

Hooray! We did it! The parts of speech are all there!

● ●

Parts of Speech in Action

By themselves, parts of speech don't go anywhere. They're just a list of things. But when we put them to work in sentences, something begins to happen.

To sort out the different jobs, we give them additional names, such as **subject** and **predicate**. The subject is *who* or *what* the sentence is about. The predicate is everything else; it explains or describes what the subject is doing.

The quick brown fox **jumped over the lazy dog's back.**
       subject   predicate

As you can see, the subject includes several parts of speech. Ditto for the predicate. Let's take a closer look at both.

Subject

The **subject** is what the sentence is about. It answers questions such as *Who* did something? or *What* happened?

Time flies.   **Dracula** scares the pants off people.
subject   subject

What flies? Time.
Who scares the pants off people? Dracula.

The subject can be a single word (Dracula) or a phrase (the story of Count Dracula).

The story of Count Dracula scares the pants off people.
subject

A **simple subject** is the main noun or pronoun *without* any of the other words that go with it.

The **vampire** with the very long teeth gazed at my throat.
simple subject

A **complete subject** is the simple subject *plus* any words that modify the subject.

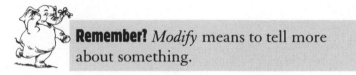

Remember? *Modify* means to tell more about something.

The vampire with the very long teeth gazed at my throat.
complete subject

Predicate

The **predicate** says something about what the subject is or is doing.

Important! A predicate always includes a verb.

Time **flies.**　　Danielle **daydreams**.
predicate　　　　　　　predicate

Dracula **scares** the pants off people.
predicate

Just as there are simple and complete subjects, there are simple and complete predicates. A **simple predicate** is just the verb. (The underlined words above are simple predicates.) A **complete predicate** is every single thing that isn't part of the complete subject.

Time **flies when you're having fun**.
  complete predicate

Danielle **daydreams of winning a medal in gymnastics when she should be studying**.   complete predicate

Dracula **scares the pants off people**.
      complete predicate

Compound Subjects and Predicates

In grammar, the word *compound* means two or more words working together. A **compound subject** is two or more subjects that go with the same verb.

> **The quick brown fox and the lazy dog** jumped over the armadillo.   compound subject

A **compound predicate** is two or more predicates that have the same subject.

> The startled armadillo **yelped and rolled into a ball**.
>   compound predicate

Understood Subjects and Predicates

If the subject or predicate isn't actually written out, it's "understood." Suppose a sentence is an order.

> Answer the question.

Who's answering? You are. "You" is understood to be the subject.

Understood predicates are similar. They aren't written out, but you understand their meaning as if they were.

Who ate the chocolate chip cookies? Your big sister.

The understood predicate in the second sentence is "ate the chocolate chip cookies."

I *understood* that she ate my cookies!

More about Verbs

Verbs have different forms. *Fly, flies, flew, flown,* and *flying* are all forms of the verb *to fly*.

The reason you change a verb from one form to another is to show the following:

All those at once?

- ✓ Number
- ✓ Person
- ✓ Voice
- ✓ Tense

That's a lot of terms to understand, so let's take them one by one.

Number

shows if a word is *singular* (only one of something) or *plural* (more than one).

> **Important!** In fact, the only place where verbs change to show number is the present tense of the third person singular: she thinks, he thinks, *but* they think (*not* they thinks).

That sounds complicated, but the table on the next page shows how it works.

Person tells who is the speaker, who is spoken to, and who is spoken about. It determines which verb and pronoun to use.

✓ **First person** is *I* (singular) or *we* (plural); this is the person speaking.

✓ **Second person** is *you* (both singular and plural); this is the person spoken *to*.

✓ **Third person** is *he, she, it* (singular), and *they* (plural); this is the person spoken *about*.

For example, if you're writing about yourself, you use the first person, *I,* and the form of the verb that goes with first person: *I dance*.

	Singular	**Plural**
1st Person	I dance	we dance
2nd Person	you dance	you dance
3rd Person	**he, she, it dances**	they dance

As you can see, the only place where the verb changes is in the third person singular.

Voice shows whether the subject of the verb is acting (**active voice**) or being acted upon (**passive voice**).

Active Voice: Celeste is assembling a computer. (The subject, Celeste, is doing the assembling.)

Passive Voice: The computer is being assembled by Celeste. (The subject, computer, is being acted upon.)

Active Voice: I burned the toast.

Passive Voice: The toast was burned by me.

Tense

Tense tells *when an action is happening:* in the present (now), in the past, or in the future.

Singular	Present	Past	Future
1st Person	I dance	I danced	I will dance
2nd Person	you dance	you danced	you will dance
3rd Person	he, she, it dances	he, she, it danced	he, she, it will dance

Plural	Present	Past	Future
1st Person	we dance	we danced	we will dance
2nd Person	you dance	you danced	you will dance
3rd Person	they dance	they danced	they will dance

Sometimes main verbs need help with tenses; they get the help they need from (ta-dum!) **helping verbs.** You can see how it's done in the future tense (above) and in the following example:

> We **will dance** all night. (future tense)
> helping main
> verb   verb

Helping verbs are also called **auxiliary verbs.** They save you the trouble of changing the main verb when you want to show past or future. Instead, you just change the tense of the helping verb.

Here are all twenty-three helping verbs.

am   are   be   been   being   is   was   were

Important! The eight verbs above are all forms of *to be.*

can, could   would, should
do, does, did   has, have, had
may, might, must   shall, will

A main verb can have more than one helping verb.

I **may** **have** **giggled**.
helping helping   main

I **might** **have** **had** the hiccups.
helping helping   main

The **progressive tense** shows an action that's still going on.

I **am dancing**.

I **have been dancing** for hours.

I **will be dancing** tomorrow.

Stop that dancing up there!

Regular and Irregular Verbs

Verbs such as *dance* and *sneeze* are called **regular verbs**. To change a regular verb into the past tense, you add *-d* or *-ed* to the present tense. Most verbs are regular verbs.

Present: I sneeze   they giggle
Past: I sneezed   they giggled

We call verbs that change to the past tense in other ways **irregular verbs**. Some irregular verbs change a vowel.

I sw**i**m every day at the YMCA.
I sw**a**m there yesterday.
I have sw**u**m there for years.
(*Have* is one of those **helping verbs**.)

Some irregular verbs change a final *-d* to *-t*.

> Please **send** me a secret message.
> I **sent** it an hour ago.
> I have already **sent** it twice.

Some don't change at all.

> I **read** Spanish easily.
> Yesterday I **read** a book in Spanish.
> I have **read** several books this month.

Compare the regular and irregular verbs on both pages 28 and 29. As you can see, verbs have three main forms (often called their principal parts): **present tense, past tense,** and **past participle.**

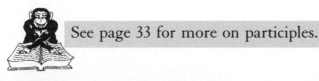

Parti-whatle?

Oops—another term! Maybe the easiest way to understand participles is to look at the two jobs they do.

✓ Participles help show tense.
✓ Participles act as adjectives.

See page 33 for more on participles.

Here, we're concerned with Job #1, showing tense. The **past participle** is used with *have* or *had* to form the perfect tenses: **present perfect, past perfect,** and **future perfect.** The following sentences illustrate each of the perfect tenses.

Present Perfect: I **have flown** kites for years.
Past Perfect: I **had flown** kites long before I learned to ski.
Future Perfect: I **will have flown** kites in every state by the time I'm twenty-one.

Let's look at the principal parts of both irregular and regular verbs.

Irregular verbs are, well, irregular! However, you probably know most of them without even thinking about it.

Five of the verbs in the table below have the same past tense and past participle. Can you find them?

Principal Parts of Irregular Verbs

Present Today I . . .	Past Yesterday I . . .	Past Participle Before that, I have . . .
am (we are)	was (we were)	been (we have been)
begin	began	begun
break	broke	broken
bring	brought	brought
choose	chose	chosen
drink	drank	drunk
eat	ate	eaten
forget	forgot	forgotten
get	got	gotten
go	went	gone
hold	held	held
know	knew	known
lie	lay	lain
ride	rode	ridden
run	ran	run
say	said	said
shake	shook	shaken
slide	slid	slid
swim	swam	swum
take	took	taken
think	thought	thought
throw	threw	thrown
write	wrote	written

Answer: The five verbs with the same past tense and past participle are *bring, hold, say, slide,* and *think.*

Principal Parts of Regular Verbs

Present Today I...	Past Yesterday I...	Past Participle Before that I have...
chew	chewed	chewed
climb	climbed	climbed
wiggle	wiggled	wiggled

The perfect tense is something you've used a lot but didn't know it had a name. The examples will help you figure it out.

The **present perfect tense** is an action started in the past that's either just completed or is still going on.

> I **have laughed** myself silly watching *The Three Stooges*.

The **past perfect tense** is an action that was started in the past and completed in the past.

> I **had laughed** myself silly by the time Larry hit Curly with a lemon pie.

The **future perfect tense** is an action that will be started and finished at a specific time in the future.

> By the end of the movie, I **will have laughed** myself silly for two hours.

(Continued on page 30)

Singular	Present Perfect	Past Perfect	Future Perfect
1st Person	I have danced	I had danced	I will have danced
2nd Person	you have danced	you had danced	you will have danced
3rd Person	he, she, it has danced	he, she, it had danced	he, she, it will have danced

Plural	Present Perfect	Past Perfect	Future Perfect
1st Person	we have danced	we had danced	we will have danced
2nd Person	you have danced	you had danced	you will have danced
3rd Person	they have danced	they had danced	they will have danced

Linking Verbs

Linking verbs connect subjects with the rest of sentences. They are often a form of *to be*.

> is, am, are, were, was

They may also be "sense" verbs.

> feel, look, sound, taste, smell

Verbs such as *become, continue, remain,* and *seem* are also linking verbs.

> **Linda was dizzy.**
> subject linking predicate
>   verb
>
> **Geraldo feels sleepy.**
> subject linking predicate
>   verb

Linking verbs are *not* action verbs. They do not take objects.

> **Action Verb:** I **read** books. (*Books* is the object of *read*.)
> **Linking Verb:** The book **seems** difficult. (There is no object.)

In the sentences below, the verb *looks* is an action verb in one sentence and a linking verb in the other. Which is the linking verb? How can you tell?

I know, I know!

Oswald looks worried.
Oswald looks at the picture.

Verb Forms

As if they weren't troublesome enough already, sometimes verbs invade the turf of other parts of speech. Then, of course, we have to give them new names! Verbs that act like nouns, adjectives, or adverbs are called **infinitives, gerunds,** and **participles**.

Infinitives combine a verb and the word *to*.

> to fly   to dance   to skateboard   to study

Infinitives can act as adverbs, adjectives, or nouns.

As an adverb: I want *to fly* my prize-winning kite.

The infinitive *to fly* modifies the verb *want;* it describes what I want.

As a noun: *To fly* a three-person kite is my dream.

The infinitive *to fly* is the subject of the verb *is*.

As an adjective: For a real challenge, the kite *to fly* is a stunt kite.

The infinitive *to fly* tells which kite is being described; it's modifying the noun *kite*.

Answer: It's the first one. It doesn't have an object.

You create a **split infinitive** when you put a word between the verb and *to,* as in "to boldly go." Split infinitives used to be frowned on, but now they are usually accepted. However, sometimes removing the split improves writing.

> **Awkward:** A told B to not eat so much pizza.
> **Better:** A told B not to eat so much pizza.

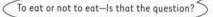
To eat or not to eat—Is that the question?

Important! We use the word *to* in two ways:

✓ As part of an infinitive (*to fly*)
✓ As a preposition (*to the moon*)

I'd like **to fly to the moon**.
infinitive prepositional phrase

Gerund is the name we give to verbs when they end in *-ing* and act as if they were nouns.

> **Playing** soccer **takes** coordination.
>   gerund   verb

The main verb in this sentence is *takes,* not *playing.* The gerund *playing* is part of the complete subject: *playing soccer.* As a subject, it is doing the job of a noun.

> **Eating** crackers in bed is a crummy idea.
>   gerund

YUM!

Thinking is the hardest work there is, which is probably why
   gerund
so few people do it.

                                                    —Henry Ford

Participles are verb forms with two different jobs.

1. As an adjective:

When participles act as adjectives, they end in *-ing, -d, -ed, -en,* or *-t.*

> *broken* kite   *burning* question   *whipped* cream
> *dancing* shoes   *burnt* toast   *breaking* news

2. As a way to show tense:

In this job, participles combine with **auxiliary,** or **helping, verbs.**

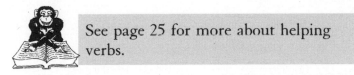

See page 25 for more about helping verbs.

I **might have flown** my kite.   I **am flying** my kite.
   helping   participle   helping participle
   verb   verb

I **had flown** my kite.   I **will be flying** my kite.
   helping participle   helping   participle
   verb   verb

A **participial phrase** combines a participle and its modifiers.

The **spaceship, lurching wildly, approached** the runway.
   subject   participial phrase   predicate

You should stick to kites.

More about Pronouns

Pronouns are grouped according to how they are used in a sentence. There are five groups: **personal, relative, demonstrative, indefinite,** and **interrogative**.

Personal pronouns are the pronouns we use the most.

Singular: I, me, you, he, him, she, her, it
Plural: us, you, they, them
Possessive: my, mine, her, hers, his, your, yours, their, theirs, its

Personal pronouns stand in for a noun. Three things determine which pronoun you should use.

✓ Case
✓ Person
✓ Number

Maybe you're beginning to recognize some of these terms now—we met two of them (person and number) in the preceding section about verbs. Again, if you just stick with me, I think the terms will become clear.

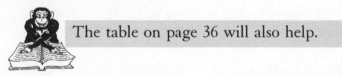

The table on page 36 will also help.

Case

The job a pronoun does in a sentence determines which case to use. It's a lot simpler than it sounds. Take a look at this sentence.

Me owes **she** ten dollars.

Me and *she* are both perfectly good personal pronouns, but they aren't in the *right case*. When the pronouns are in the right case, the sentence would look like this.

> I owe **her** ten dollars.

Here's how it works. There are three cases: **nominative, objective,** and **possessive**. When the pronoun is the subject, use the **nominative case**. Examples: *I, we, you, he, she, it, they.*

> I fly kites. (*Not* **Me** fly kites.)

I is the subject of the verb *fly*.

When the pronoun is an object, use the **objective case**. Examples: *me, us, her, him, them*.

> Give **me** the kite.

Me is the indirect object of the verb *give*.

Note: *You* and *it* are the same in the nominative and objective cases.

Which of these sentences is right?

> Me and Juan went to the mall.
> Juan and me went to the mall.
> Juan and I went to the mall.

To help you decide, get rid of Juan. Now which would you choose?

> Me ~~and Juan~~ went to the mall.
> ~~Juan and~~ me went to the mall.
> ~~Juan and~~ I went to the mall.

You wouldn't say "Me went to the mall," so *I* is clearly the right choice. *I* is the subject of the sentence, so you use the nominative case.

Which of the following sentences is correct?

> Give the money to Juan and I.
> Give the money to Juan and me.

Again, remove "Juan and" to help you decide. Would you say, "Give the money to I"? No, so the second sentence is correct. Why? Because *me* is an object of the preposition *to,* and pronouns that are objects should be in the objective case; *me* is in the objective case (see the table of pronouns below).

When a personal pronoun shows possession, it tells *who* or *what* something belongs to; use the **possessive case** for these pronouns. Examples: *mine, ours, theirs.*

> The Sky Tiger kite is **mine**.

Possessive pronouns can be in front of a noun (*my* toothache, *his* big toe) or can stand by themselves (This eraser is *yours*.).

	Nominative	Objective	Possessive
1st Person	I, we	me, us	my, mine, our, ours
2nd Person	you	you	your, yours
3rd Person	he, she, it, they	him, her, them, it	his, her, hers, its, their, theirs

Person

Person shows who is *the speaker,* who is *spoken to,* and who is *spoken about.* The speaker is the **first person** (*I, we*). The person spoken *to* is the **second person** (*you*). The person or thing spoken *about* is the **third person** (*he, she, it, they*). The table of pronouns above groups pronouns by both case and person. Use this table to help you choose the right pronoun.

Number

When the pronoun replaces *one* person or thing, use a singular pronoun (*I, me, you, she, he, it*). When the pronoun replaces *more than one* person or thing, use a plural pronoun (*we, you, they, them*). Note: The pronoun *you* can be either singular or plural.

Reflexive and intensive pronouns are personal

pronouns that end in *-self* or *-selves* (*myself, themselves, yourself*). The pronoun is called **reflexive** when it refers to someone or something already mentioned.

> **Reflexive:** I hurt **myself** when I fell off the roof.

The pronoun is called **intensive** when it shows emphasis.

> **Intensive:** I will fly the kite **myself!**

Use pronouns like *myself* or *herself* only for emphasis or when you're referring to something or someone already mentioned.

> **Wrong:** Give the kite to Gina and **myself**.
> **Right:** Give the kite to Gina and **me**.

Relative pronouns are connecting words. The com-

monly used relative pronouns are *who, whom, which, that, whoever, whomever, whose,* and *what*.

> The kite **that** has a purple tail was caught in a tree.

The relative pronoun *that* connects the kite and its tail; *that* is also the subject of the verb *has*.

My tail is well connected!

The witch **who** sings off-key is wearing a pointy hat.

Who connects the word *witch* with *sings off-key*. *Who* is also the subject of the verb *sings*.

Who is used when the pronoun is a subject. *Whom* is used when the pronoun is the object of a verb or preposition.

> who = nominative case
> whom = objective case

To help you decide whether to use *who* or *whom,* substitute a personal pronoun for the word. If *I, she, he,* or *they* sounds right, use *who* (nominative case).

> The witch **who** sings off-key... (*She* sings off-key, not *her* sings off-key.)

If *me, him, her,* or *them* sounds right, use *whom* (objective case).

> Molly, with **whom** I have an annual bet on the Super Bowl,... (I have an annual bet with *her,* not with *she.*)

Demonstrative pronouns point to people or things; like adjectives, they show which one: *this* tattoo, *that* banana, *these* eggs, *those* volleyball players.

Demonstrative pronouns can also refer to something said earlier.

> Clementine didn't buy any property; **that** is no way to win Monopoly.

The demonstrative pronoun *that* refers to "not buying any property."

Don't use *that* unless it directly follows what it's referring to.

> **Wrong:** I'm not **that** hungry.
> **Right:** Tanya ate twelve pancakes, but I'm not **that** hungry.

Indefinite pronouns, as their name suggests, are rather vague. Examples are *any, all, several, few, some, each, every,* and compounds with *-body, -thing,* and *-one* (such as *no one, everyone, somebody, something, nobody, nothing*).

> **Nobody** is to leave this room.
> **Everyone** is in the class play.

Interrogative pronouns indicate questions: *who, whom, which, what,* and *whose.*

> **Whose** backpack is this?
> **Who** left the refrigerator open?
> **What** happened?
> **Who** gave **what** to **whom**?
> **Which** is the right answer?

I don't know!

Important! Use *who* when it's the subject; use *whom* when it's the object of a verb or preposition.

> **Who** helped <u>**whom**</u>?
> subject   object of verb

The Building Blocks of Sentences

What is a sentence? How do we put one together? First, we take words and put them into phrases and clauses; then we put the phrases and clauses together to make sentences.

Looks like we need to define some more terms. A **phrase** is a group of words with no subject or predicate. This means that, by itself, a phrase is never a complete sentence.

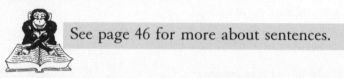

See page 46 for more about sentences.

Phrases can act as different parts of speech.

> **Noun Phrase: The stubborn gray mule** was wearing a straw hat.
> **Adverb Phrase: While hanging by my knees**, I recited the multiplication tables.
> **Adjective Phrase:** My favorite activity, **playing a complicated computer game**, can be played with a friend.
> **Preposition Phrase:** I fell asleep **under the weeping willow tree**.

Phrases by themselves are good for dramatic emphasis.

> Over my dead body!

I occasionally use them in this book to answer questions.

> What are subject and verb supposed to agree about? **Being either singular or plural.**   phrase

OVER MY
DEAD
BODY!

Unlike a phrase, a **clause** has a subject and a predicate. If a clause expresses a complete thought, it's called an **independent clause**.

A sentence that consists only of an independent clause is called a **simple sentence**.

Simple Sentence: <u>**I fly my stunt kite on Wednesdays**</u>.
independent clause

Two independent clauses joined by a conjunction are called a **compound sentence**.

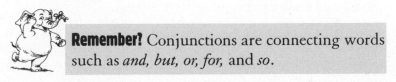

Remember? Conjunctions are connecting words such as *and, but, or, for,* and *so.*

Compound Sentence:
<u>**I fly my stunt kite on Wednesdays,**</u> **but** <u>**I play soccer on Fridays**</u>.
independent clause   conjunction   independent clause

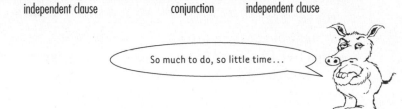

So much to do, so little time...

A **dependent (subordinate) clause** is not a complete thought. For example, the dependent clause "When I'm not flying kites" is not a complete thought because we don't know what happens when I'm not flying kites. It needs an independent clause to complete the thought. A sentence made up of both a dependent and an independent clause is called a **complex sentence**.

Complex sentence:
<u>**When I'm not flying kites,**</u> <u>**I'm repairing spaceships**</u>.
dependent clause   independent clause

Phrases and clauses are called **restrictive** if they are needed for the meaning of a word or sentence. They are **nonrestrictive** if they just add information that you don't absolutely have to have.

Restrictive: The kite **with the purple tail** belongs to Analisa.

To be able to tell which kite is Analisa's, you have to know it's the one with the purple tail. That information is essential.

Nonrestrictive: Analisa's box kite, **which she made from balsa wood and tissue paper,** won first prize.

You don't need to know what Analisa made the kite from to understand that her kite won first prize. It's nice to have the information, but it's not essential.

Use commas to separate the **nonrestrictive phrase** from the rest of the sentence; don't use commas with **restrictive phrases**.

Sentences are also described as **declarative, interrogative, imperative**, and **exclamatory**.

A **declarative sentence** makes a statement.

> I fly kites.

An **interrogative sentence** asks a question.

> Do you fly kites?

An **imperative sentence** gives an order.

> Go fly a kite!

An **exclamatory sentence** expresses a strong feeling.

> Flying kites is exhilarating!

Now that you've crammed your cranium full of useful terms, let's look at some of the ways to **write right**!

3

What You Need to Know about Grammar

●●●●●●●●●●●●●●●●●●●●●●●●●●●●

The Rules of Grammar

Using grammar is like driving a car. When everyone knows and follows the rules (which side of the road to drive on, what traffic lights mean, and so on), there are fewer bent fenders. In the same way, communication proceeds smoothly when you follow the rules of grammar.

There are only a few such rules, and their aim is to make writing logical. Here are some of the main ones.

- ✓ Put modifiers where they won't be confusing.
- ✓ Use plural verbs with plural subjects.
- ✓ Use singular verbs with singular subjects.

There's not much more to grammar than that. The tricky part is knowing **how and where to apply the rules**. Where *do* modifiers belong? How can you tell if a subject is singular or plural?

To help sort out the rules, I've put the most important ones in six groups. You can look up any terms you don't know in the glossary at the back of the book.

Hey, that sounds easy!

Avoid Faulty Sentences

Those grammarians I mentioned earlier came up with the term *sentence fault* to describe two common writing errors: fragments and run-ons.

A **fragment** has two important features: It's missing either a subject or main verb, and it isn't a complete thought.

A **run-on** is the opposite. It crams too much into one sentence. In particular, a run-on squeezes two independent clauses into a sentence and separates them only by a comma or by no punctuation at all.

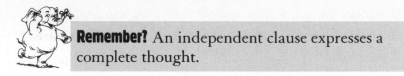

Remember? An independent clause expresses a complete thought.

To sort these out, let's look at examples of both fragments and run-ons.

Fragment: While we were watching the movie.

At first, you might see the words *we* and *were watching* and think the fragment has a subject and verb. But notice how it feels unfinished; you're still waiting to find out *what happened*.

Fixed: While we were watching the movie, we ate ten bags of popcorn.

How to Fix Fragments

To fix a fragment, you need to supply what's missing. That means adding a subject or a main verb or completing the thought that you started.

✓ Add a subject.

> **Fragment:** Trying to act nonchalant and innocent.
> **Fixed:** Trying to act nonchalant and innocent, Lee slipped a piece of broccoli into her milk.

✓ Add a main verb.

> **Fragment:** Her mother, who saw her do it.
> **Fixed:** Her mother, who saw her do it, said, "Gotcha!"

✓ Complete the thought.

> **Fragment:** When your mom is mad at your dad.
> **Fixed:** When your mom is mad at your dad, don't let her brush your hair.

Are fragments always wrong? No, they can be handy tools for careful writers. For example, they are good for dialogue, since people don't always talk in complete sentences. And they are useful in a question-and-answer format.

Will they win? Not if we can help it.

But too many fragments make writing choppy, so use them only now and then, for emphasis.

Now let's look at run-ons.

Run-on: <u>It's fun to fly my stunt kite, I just learned how to stall it.</u>
independent clause   independent clause

Run-on: Seymour can make bagels, they taste great!

A comma provides only a short pause or separation; what you need between two independent clauses is a stronger break. A semicolon provides enough separation if the two clauses are closely related. If you want an even stronger feeling of separation, use a period.

See page 72 (commas), page 86 (semicolons), and page 82 (periods). Whew!

Correct: It's fun to fly my stunt kite; I just learned how to stall it.
Correct: Seymour can make bagels. They taste great!

Run-on: Learn from the mistakes of others you can't live long enough to make them all yourself.
Correct: Learn from the mistakes of others. You can't live long enough to make them all yourself.

Run-on: My sister likes to go fishing however she can't find time for it now that she's a firefighter.

Correct: My sister likes to go fishing; however, she can't find time for it now that she's a firefighter.

How to Repair Run-ons

First, find where one independent clause ends and the next one begins.

Run-on: I saw a spotted iguana it was asleep in the sun.
Separated: I saw a spotted iguana   it was asleep in the sun.

Then choose one of the following ways to correct the run-on:

✓ Separate the two parts with a semicolon.

I saw the spotted iguana; it was asleep in the sun.

✓ Separate the two parts with a period.

I saw the spotted iguana. It was asleep in the sun.

✓ Separate the two parts with a comma and add a conjunction to the second part.

I saw the spotted iguana, **but** it was asleep in the sun.
conjunction

✓ Add a conjunction to the first part and separate the two parts with a comma.

When I saw the spotted iguana, it was asleep in the sun.
conjunction

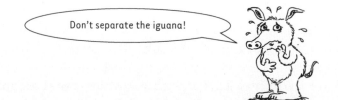

Don't separate the iguana!

Make References Clear

When you refer to something, you point at it. Modifiers and pronouns refer to other words. It's important to make them point at those words carefully. Here are some problems to watch for and ways to correct them.

Avoid misplaced modifiers.

You probably remember that modifiers tell us more about a word or phrase. If you put them in the wrong spot, they are "misplaced." In other words, they are misplaced if they aren't pointing carefully at the words they modify.

Misplaced Modifier:
I saw a man on a horse **with a wooden leg**.

misplaced modifier

See what I mean? It looks like the horse, not the man, has the wooden leg. In order to be clear, the modifier should be close to the words it modifies. So, let's try again.

Better:
I saw a man **with a wooden leg** on a horse.

Even with that improvement, you might still misinterpret this sentence. Let's try one more time.

Right: I saw a man **with a wooden leg** riding on a horse.

Now look back at the sentence we began with and see how we changed a grammatical goof into a healthy sentence. All we did was move the phrase *with a wooden leg* and add one word, *riding*. That wasn't hard, was it? But it changes the sentence from one that readers will laugh at to one they will understand.

Here are some other examples of grammatical goofs. Cover up the corrected sentences before you look at them; see if you can correct the sentences yourself.

> **Misplaced Modifier:** Denzel was hit by a fastball that required eight stitches.

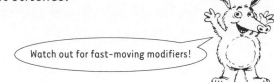

Watch out for fast-moving modifiers!

What required eight stitches? Presumably a cut, which isn't even mentioned in the sentence.

> **Correct:** When Denzel was hit by a fastball, the cut on his head required eight stitches.
>
> **Misplaced Modifier:** The protesters were carried out by the police on stretchers.
>
> **Correct:** The protesters were carried out on stretchers by the police.
>
> **Correct:** The police carried out the protesters on stretchers.

Sometimes the misplaced modifier is not a phrase but a single word. The word *almost* in the following sentence is misplaced.

> **Misplaced Modifier:** The bicycle spokes were **almost bent so badly** that they couldn't be straightened.

The spokes were not *almost* bent, they were *actually* bent. Move *almost* so that it modifies *couldn't be straightened*.

> **Correct:** The bicycle spokes were bent so badly that they **almost couldn't be straightened**.

Avoid dangling modifiers.

Dangling modifiers is a funny term. It describes phrases that "dangle" at the beginning of a sentence; the words they modify aren't where they belong, which is right after the phrase.

> **Dangling Modifier: Being old and dog-eared,** the teacher was able to buy the book for one dollar.

The book, not the teacher, is what's old and dog-eared. The phrase *being old and dog-eared* dangles because what it modifies (*book*) should be next to it instead of later in the sentence. Rewrite the sentence to bring them together.

> **Clear:** Since the book was old and dog-eared, the teacher was able to buy it for one dollar.

> **Dangling Modifier: Reading the sentence slowly,** the misspelled word was found.

It sounds as if the misspelled word was reading the sentence. Who did the reading? That's the subject you need to add so that the opening phrase isn't left dangling.

> **Clear:** Reading the sentence slowly, Latasha found the misspelled word.

Make pronouns refer clearly to their antecedents.

This rule helps you use pronouns correctly, which is also important in clear writing. The new term here is **antecedent**. An antecedent is the noun that is referred to by a pronoun; it's what the pronoun replaces.

> I gave Marisela my **baseball cards;** I gave **them** to her
> because she is my best friend. ↑   ↑
>   antecedent   pronoun

The pronoun *them* refers to (replaces) the antecedent *baseball cards*. There are other pronouns in the sentence. How many can you find? What are their antecedents?

How about the antecedent in the following sentence?

> Malcolm told Jay, and then he told me.

Who told me, Malcolm or Jay? It's not clear, so rewrite the sentence to remove the confusion.

> Malcolm first told Jay and then told me.

In a well-written sentence, a lot of words may come between a pronoun and its antecedent, but the word the pronoun refers to is clear.

> The *tongue* weighs almost nothing, but few people can hold *it*.

My Aunty Cedent came before me.

Answer: The six other pronouns are *I*, *my*, *I*, *her*, *she*, and *my*. The antecedent for *I* and *my* is Jan Venolia (or whoever is speaking). The antecedent for *her* and *she* is Marisela.

Go for Agreement

In grammar, agreement isn't between people deciding what movie to go to or which pizza to order. It's between subjects and verbs or between pronouns and their antecedents.

What are they supposed to agree about? Being either singular or plural. That's their "number." The examples below will help you get the idea.

Remember? Singular means one; plural means more than one.

Make subject and verb agree in number.

This is one of the most important rules of grammar, so let's take it apart and see what it means. *Agree in number* means using a singular verb with a singular subject and a plural verb with a plural subject.

Subject	Singular	Plural
Subject	person	people
Verb	is	are

If the subject is singular, like *person,* use a singular verb, such as *is*.
If the subject is plural, like *person,* use a plural verb, such as *are*.

So far, so good. But first you have to *find the subject,* and then you have to *decide whether it's singular or plural*. That's when things can get complicated. Let's look at those two jobs, one at a time.

What's the Subject?

Take a sentence such as the following:

The loss of my two favorite box kites was a blow.

The verb is easy to find: It's *was*. But the word directly in front of the verb is *kites*. Is that the subject? No. *Kites* is the object of the preposition *of*. It tells us more about the subject, but it isn't the subject itself. The subject of the sentence is *loss* (the loss was a blow). That's what the sentence is about.

So here's our first rule on the agreement of subject and verb.

• Words or phrases that come between subject and verb do not affect the number of the verb.

The **loss** of my two favorite box kites **was** a blow.
    singular subject   singular verb

When you find the subject and the verb, just skip over any words between them. Give a singular subject a singular verb and a plural subject a plural verb.

One in five kites **is** homemade.
  singular subject   singular verb

A **handful** of stars **is** hard to catch.
   singular subject   singular verb

Five of the kites entered in the contest **were** box kites.
  plural subject   plural verb

Here's our second rule to help make subject and verb agree.

• If the subject of a sentence is a phrase or clause, use a singular verb.

Examples help explain this rule.

<u>**The best way to keep your friends**</u> **is** not to give them away.
subject = phrase   sing.
                                verb

<u>**Having six puppies**</u> **is** a lot of work.
subject = phrase   sing.
                        verb

<u>**Talking in class**</u> **gets** you in trouble.
subject = phrase   sing.
                      verb

Sometimes the verb comes before the subject. Again, first find the subject, and then decide whether to make the verb singular or plural.

Leading the list of soccer players **was** <u>**Jack B. Nimble**</u>.
                                    sing.   singular subject
                                    verb

Leading the list of soccer players
were <u>**Jack B. Nimble and Jack B. Quick**</u>.
plural   plural subject
verb

What's the Number of the Subject?

Sometimes it's not easy to tell. Here are some ways to help you decide.

Compound Subject: When a subject consists of two or more nouns joined by *and, or,* or *nor,* it's called a **compound subject**.

• When the compound subject is joined by *and,* use a plural verb.

<u>**Ice cream and pickles**</u> **taste** funny together.
compound subject   plural verb

Ice cream and hot fudge, on the other hand . . .

- When a compound subject is joined by *or* or *nor* instead of *and,* use a singular verb.

> **A passport or tourist card is** necessary for space travel.
>   compound subject   sing.
>   verb

- When the word *each* or *every* comes **before** a compound or plural subject, use a singular verb.

> **Every** UFO and alien sighting **is** studied carefully.
>   singular verb

- When the word *each* or *every* comes **after** a compound or plural subject, use a plural verb.

> UFOs and alien sightings **each have** faithful believers.
>   plural verb

- Still another kind of compound subject includes *either/or* or *neither/nor*. In that case, make the verb agree with the nearest noun.

> Neither Jack nor **Jill is** carrying a pail of water.
>   singular sing.
>   subject   verb
>
> Neither Jack nor the **twins are** carrying pails of water.
>   plural   plural
>   subject   verb

Collective Nouns: Collective nouns describe a group or collection; some examples are *family, group, people, percent,* and *team*.

- Collective nouns take a singular verb if they refer to the group as a whole.

> The **group is meeting** tonight to discuss UFOs.
>   coll.   singular verb
>   noun
>
> The whole **family wants** to go to the movies.
>   coll.   singular verb
>   noun

- If the collective noun refers to individuals within the group, use a plural verb.

The **people** on the spaceship **were floating** in zero gravity.
coll.   plural verb
noun

Sometimes the subject is *a sum or quantity* (say, five dollars or ten minutes). If the sum or quantity is thought of as a single unit, it takes a singular verb. This is true even if the subject is plural.

Twenty dollars **is** a good price for a used bike.
sum   sing.
verb

The number of the noun **following a fraction** determines the number of the verb.

Three-fourths of the **coins** **have been** counted.
plural   plural verb

Three-fourths of the **money** **is missing**.
singular   singular verb

Make pronoun and antecedent agree in number.

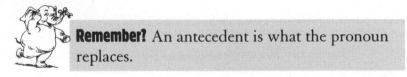

Remember? An antecedent is what the pronoun replaces.

Logic tells us that if you have a singular antecedent (*rabbit*), you refer to it with a singular pronoun (*it*); if you have a plural antecedent (*rabbits*), you refer to it with a plural pronoun (*they* or *them*).

I have a pet **rabbit,** but I think **it** is lonely.
singular   singular
antecedent   pronoun

If I had two **rabbits, they** would keep each other company.
plural   plural
antecedent pronoun

What does this have to do with good writing? If readers don't know what a pronoun refers to (in other words, what its antecedent is), they will be confused. You want your writing to be clear, not confusing.

Confusing: The talkative **student** will get detention if **they** aren't careful.   singular antecedent   plural
pronoun

Clear: Talkative students will get detention if **they** aren't careful.
plural antecedent   plural pronoun

But here's a problem. When people follow this rule and make singular antecedents and pronouns agree, they sometimes write a sentence such as this:

Each contestant must provide **his** own stunt kite.
singular antecedent   singular pronoun

When a masculine pronoun is used for both masculine and feminine, girls and women might feel left out. Writing is considered biased if it addresses only male readers.

What should you do about this? One popular solution for removing bias is to use both masculine and feminine pronouns.

Each **contestant** must provide **his or her** own stunt kite.
singular antecedent   singular pronouns

But that's clumsy. Here are some better ways to remove bias.

• Make the antecedent plural and use the plural pronoun *their*.

Neutral: The **contestants** must provide **their** own stunt kites.
plural antecedent   plural pronoun

- Write in the second person (*you*) instead of the third person (*he, she*).

> **Neutral:** Bring **your** books to class.
> 2nd person

- Remove pronouns that aren't needed.

> **Awkward:** Each student must turn in **his or her** book report by Thursday.
> **Better:** Each student must turn in **a** book report by Thursday.

> **Awkward:** Did anyone lose **his or her** glasses?
> **Better:** Did anyone lose **a pair of** glasses?

As you can see, you have lots of ways to write so that no one feels left out. It's a good idea to make bias-free writing so automatic that you don't even have to think about it.

Now everybody is included!

Use Parallel Construction

Use parallel words to express parallel thoughts.

> **Unparallel:** Give me liberty or kill me.
> **Parallel:** Give me liberty or give me death.

> **Unparallel:** I like flying kites, going to the mall, and to swim.
> **Parallel:** I like flying kites, going to the mall, and swimming.

Got the idea? Once you've established a pattern (such as a series of phrases or action verbs), stick with that pattern.

Use Articles Correctly

Remember? Articles are the words *a, an,* and *the.*

There are two kinds of articles: definite and indefinite. The **definite article** is *the;* it shows that the noun is not just any book or apple but a particular book or apple (*the* book about alien life-forms, *the* apple with a worm hole). The **indefinite articles** are *a* and *an;* they show that the noun is one of many things (*a* book, *an* apple).

In general, use the article *a* before words beginning with a consonant (*a* guitar, *a* NASA program); use *an* before words that either begin with a vowel (*an* eagle) or are pronounced with a vowel sound (*an* NBA ruling).

Remember? Do you remember what vowels and consonants are? Vowels are *a, e, i, o, u,* and sometimes *y.* All other letters are consonants.

The **a/an** rule (*a* before consonants, *an* before vowels) needs to be fine-tuned. The letter *h* is a consonant that we pronounce in two ways: (1) We give it a breathy sound (called *aspirating*) in words like *history* and *helicopter;* (2) we don't pronounce it at all in *hour* and *honest.* When the *h* is aspirated, use the article *a* (*a hysterical viewer);* when the *h* is silent, use *an* (*an honorable mention).*

The other **a/an** problem is with acronyms such as NASA and NBA. We pronounce NASA as a word, and since the word begins with a consonant, we use *a: a NASA mission.* But we pronounce the individual letters of NBA, rather than saying it as if it were a word. Although the first letter of NBA is the consonant N, when we say "N," it sounds as if it begins with the vowel *e:* "en." So, the correct article to use is *an: an NBA ruling.*

Avoid Double Trouble

Sometimes we go overboard and end up writing something twice. Here are a couple of places where that might happen.

Watch for double negatives.

Two negatives cancel each other.

Wrong: Don't give me no trouble.

Presumably "trouble" is what you don't want, not "no trouble." So, let's remove one of the negatives.

Right: Don't give me any trouble.

Words such as *almost, barely, hardly,* or *nearly* are already negative. Don't add negative words to them.

Wrong: I couldn't hardly believe what I heard.

Remove one of the negatives.

Right: I could hardly believe what I heard.

As with many rules of grammar, this one can be stretched. Suppose you're *sort of* willing to do something. A double negative gets this idea across.

I am not unwilling to go kitesurfing, but it scares me to think of it.

Suppose you want to indicate that something is faintly possible.

It's not impossible that I will finish my homework on time.

Use such double negatives only now and then; otherwise, you give the impression that you never come straight out and say anything directly.

Avoid double comparisons.

To compare things, we use words like *more* and *most* (more turtles, most trophies) and the word endings *-er* and *-est* (kinder, kindest). If you use them at the same time, you create awkward (and incorrect) expressions like *more kinder* and *most kindest*. Use one comparison word at a time.

Wrong: This is more easier than you think it is.
Right: This is easier than you think it is.

4

What You Need to Know about Punctuation

• •

Punctuation Pointers

If grammar provides the "rules of the road" for writing, then punctuation provides the road signs: slow down here (comma), detour there (dash, parentheses), and stop (semicolon, period).

When we speak to each other, we use body language to punctuate our words. We raise or lower our voices, shake our fists, point, pause, and so on. In writing, punctuation marks do those jobs.

That doesn't mean you should load up each sentence with punctuation. Too much of it makes writing choppy. The right amount of punctuation will help readers understand your meaning.

Apostrophe ,

I think people make more mistakes with apostrophes than with any other punctuation mark. An apostrophe is often missing when it's needed and pops up where it doesn't belong.

For example, the apostrophe is missing from the following question:

Whose going to Seattle?

Wrong *whose!* The word should be *who's,* a contraction of *who is* (*Who is* going to Seattle?).

Often, the apostrophe shows up where it's not wanted.

The dog wagged it's tail.

Important! *It's* is always a contraction of *it is* or *it has*. Although we do use apostrophes to show possession in other words, the pro noun *its* is possessive *without* the addition of an apostrophe. The following sentence shows how to use *it's* and *its* correctly.

It's easy to put the apostrophe in **its** place.
It is   possessive pronoun

Well, I seem to have started with the mistakes people make when they're using apostrophes. What's the right way to use them? Apostrophes have three main jobs.

✓ To show possession
✓ To show a contraction
✓ To make letters and certain words plural

Use an apostrophe to show possession, as follows:

1. With all *singular* words, add '*s.*
2. With all *plural* words that end in *s,* add the apostrophe only.
3. With *plural* words that don't end in *s,* add '*s.*

1. Singular words (add 's)
ostrich's feathers
witness's testimony
class's assignment
puppy's food
teacher's grade book
the twin's backpack
   (one twin)
Groucho Marx's moustache
Statue of Liberty's torch

2. Plural words ending in s (add ')
ostriches' feathers
witnesses' testimony
classes' rivalry
puppies' food
teachers' conference
the twins' mother

3. Plural words not ending in *s* (add *'s*)
children's park   men's room   women's issues

The trick to making a plural word possessive is to be sure the word is plural *before* you add the apostrophe: the Joneses' house, *not* the Jones' house or the Jones's house.

Using *'s* with titles is awkward. Rewrite to avoid this.

Awkward: *Catcher in the Rye*'s ending
Better: the ending of *Catcher in the Rye*

Remember? Never, never, NEVER add an apostrophe to a possessive pronoun (*its, hers, his, theirs, yours, ours,* and *whose*). These words are ALREADY possessive.

Wrong: The apostrophe seems to have a life of it's own.
Right: The apostrophe seems to have a life of its own.

It's is a contraction of *it is* or *it has*.

Can a bee bend it's knees?
Does a dog scratch it's fleas?
No, NO, that's not right.
Pay attention now, please.

No apostrophe's needed.
That's all there is to it.
If you added one there,
Well then, you just blew it.

The bee bends its knees
You've got it—Hooray!
Remember it always,
And you'll get an A!

P.S. The dog scratches *its* fleas, too, but I couldn't figure out how to fit it into my poem! 😊

Use an apostrophe in contractions.

Contractions are words that have been shortened by leaving out some letters. Numbers are also shortened in this way.

> can't   he's   you're   Roaring '20s   summer of '05

You make contractions by squeezing two words together and replacing one or more letters with an apostrophe.

it is = it's	they are = they're
was not = wasn't	I would = I'd
we will = we'll	will not = won't

If you're contracting numbers, omit the first numbers.

'20s = 1920s	'05 = 2005

Contractions take less space than the individual words written out; they make letters to friends or family feel casual and friendly. However, they look sloppy in formal writing, so don't use contractions often in schoolwork unless they are part of dialogue or are in something you're quoting.

If you aren't sure whether you're using a contraction correctly, return the missing letters to the word and see if it makes sense.

> **Right:** You're welcome to stay for dinner.
> (*You are* welcome, not *your welcome*.)

Use an apostrophe when making letters and certain words plural.

You have to watch your **p's** and **q's** if you're going to get **A's**.

This book report has too many **and's** and **very's**.

These are special plurals that you probably won't use often.

Important! Most of the time, you make words plural by adding *-s* or *-es*, not by adding an apostrophe.

boxes, not box's   coaches, not coach's
passes, not pass's

Wrong: The three dog**'s** wagged their tail**'s**.
Right: The three dog**s** wagged their tail**s**.

Colon :

The colon tells the reader that something is coming. Look ahead.

Use a colon to introduce a list or explanation.

My spacecraft repair kit contains the following tools: monkey wrench, alligator clips, and long-nose pliers.

The words that *follow* the colon explain or provide more details about what's *before* it. Capitalize the first word following the colon *only* if it begins a complete sentence.

The prizewinning kites all had one thing in common: They were homemade.

There are three kinds of people: those who can count and those who can't.

Hey! That doesn't add up . . .

Use a colon in formal business letters.

Dear Mrs. Sippi: Dear Senator Blowhorn:

Comma ,

A comma is a good thing
To separate the clauses,
But when and where to use it
Sometimes gives me pauses.

There are many ways to use commas, but they all create separation or a pause. That means too many commas would slow readers down and make the writing choppy. On the other hand, not enough commas creates confusion. The following rules steer between those extremes.

Use a comma to separate independent clauses that are joined by the coordinating conjunctions *and, but, or, nor, for, yet,* and *so.*

 Remember? Independent clauses make complete statements; coordinating conjunctions are the words that join two independent clauses.

I have never been lost, but I will admit to being confused for several weeks.

—Daniel Boone

Unless a comma is needed to prevent misreading, you may leave it out between short closely related clauses.

Keep your face to the sunshine and you cannot see the shadow.

—Helen Keller

If the clauses are long or contain commas, separate them with a semicolon rather than a comma.

Exercise is bunk. If you are healthy, you don't need it; if you are sick, you shouldn't take it.
—Henry Ford

Use a comma after an opening subordinate clause.

Remember? A subordinate clause is not a complete thought.

If you want a kitten, start out by asking for a horse.
subordinate clause

Use commas to separate three or more items in a series.

I like pizza with black olives, pepperoni, and artichoke hearts.

A series may consist of short independent clauses.

I made the kite, I entered the contest, and I won first prize.

Use a comma between two adjectives that modify the same noun.

short, blond student   **old, dilapidated spaceship**
adjective adjective noun   adjective adjective   noun

Omit the comma when the first adjective modifies not just the noun, but the second adjective and the noun combined. That sounds a bit complicated, but some examples should help.

<u>short</u> <u>time span</u>   <u>white</u> <u>tennis shoes</u>
adjective   adjective-noun   adjective   adjective-noun
            combination   combination

Short modifies *time span,* not just *span; white* modifies *tennis shoes.*

One way to help you decide whether a comma is needed between two adjectives is to put the word *and* between them. If the phrase still makes sense, use a comma. For example, "old and dilapidated spaceship" makes sense, so you use a comma; "short and time span" doesn't make sense, so you omit the comma.

Use a comma to avoid confusion.

Someone would probably have to reread a sentence such as the following to get the right meaning:

Confusing: While the elephant ate the giraffe waited for its turn.
Clear: While the elephant ate, the giraffe waited for its turn.

Use a comma between contrasting words or phrases,

in place of conjunctions such as *but* and *though.*

The fool wonders, the wise man asks.

—Benjamin Disraeli

Use a comma to separate appositives and other nonrestrictive phrases. An appositive is a word or phrase that describes the noun that comes before it. It is called "nonrestrictive" because it adds information that is not needed to make the meaning clear.

> *Catcher in the Rye,* **a novel about growing up,** was written by J.D. Salinger. appositive

> My mother, **the family historian,** surprised me with the tale of a bank-robbing relative. ↑
> appositive

A restrictive phrase adds information that is needed. Do not use commas with restrictive phrases.

> All the students **who know how to run the school** are busy flying kites.

The restrictive phrase *who know how to run the school* is needed to tell *which* students are important, so it shouldn't be separated with commas.

Use a comma following participial phrases.

> I wish *I* knew all the answers.

> **Knowing all the answers,** I passed the test easily.

See page 33 for more about participles and participial phrases.

Use a comma when addressing someone directly.

Count Dracula, you need some breath mints.

Use a comma before quotations that are introduced by an expression such as "she said" or "he asked."

Kin Hubbard said, "A slice of eggplant makes a dandy sink stopper."

"My goose," the chef said, "is cooked."

"If you get a bad grade in school," she advised me, "show it to your mom when she's on the phone."

Use a comma after an introductory phrase or word such as *for example, that is,* or *namely*.

For example, I put a comma where it's needed in this sentence.

Use a comma after the salutations in letters to family or friends.

Dear Uncle Willie,   Dear Melissa,

Use a comma between the day and year when writing dates.

July 4, 1776

Dash ⸺

The dash is an attention-getter. Use it when you want a more emphatic break than that produced by a comma or parentheses. However, if a colon, semicolon, or comma would work just as well, use one of these instead. Too many dashes leave readers feeling sort of breathless.

The dash has a different job from that of the hyphen, which is covered on page 78. A dash is about twice as long as a hyphen.

Use a dash to emphasize, to indicate an abrupt change, or to introduce words or phrases that explain.

> *They say a reasonable number of fleas is good for a dog—keeps him from broodin' over bein' a dog.*
>
> —E. N. Westcott

> *Put all your eggs in one basket—and watch that basket!*
>
> —Mark Twain

Use a dash to summarize.

> *Nature gave us two ends—one to sit on and one to think with. Ever since then, our success or failure has depended on which one we used most.*
>
> —George R. Kirkpatrick

Use a pair of dashes to set off a phrase in the middle of a sentence, not a dash and a comma, colon, or semicolon.

Wrong: The books—all twelve of them, were overdue.
Right: The books—all twelve of them—were overdue.

Exclamation point !

Exclamation points provide punchy endings.

Use exclamation points after the following:

✓ interjections

> Ouch!

✓ exclamatory sentences

> That hurt!

✓ imperative sentences

> Don't step on my toe again!

Too many exclamation points leave a reader feeling punched out. Save them for just a few important places.

Hyphen —

Hyphens (which are about half as long as dashes) have two main jobs: (1) They hook words or parts of words together (*win-win situation, ten-foot pole*); (2) they divide words that don't fit at the end of a line. It's not always easy to know when to use a hyphen, but these rules should help.

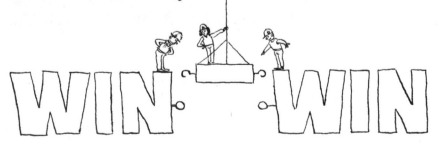

Use a hyphen with certain prefixes and suffixes.

Looks like we're back in the definition business again! A **prefix** is the part of a word that is added to the *front* of a root word; the root word is the main part of a word. In the following examples, the root words are *happy, like,* and *side.*

unhappy   **dis**like   **in**side
prefix   prefix   prefix

A **suffix** is the part of a word that is added to the *end* of a root word.

child**hood**   curios**ity**   clue**less**   cup**ful**
suffix   suffix   suffix   suffix

Use a hyphen to separate a prefix or suffix from the root word in the following cases:

✓ To avoid doubled or tripled letters

part-time   shell-like   co-owner

✓ If the root word begins with a capital letter

mid-September   sub-Saharan   Indo-European

✓ With the prefixes *all-, self-, ex-,* and *vice-*

all-purpose   self-esteem   ex-astronaut   vice-mayor

Use a hyphen to combine a capital letter with a word.

T-shirt   U-turn   G-rated

Use a hyphen with certain compound words.

Compound words combine two or more words into a single idea.

right-of-way	sit-in
stick-in-the-mud	editor-in-chief

Use hyphens with a compound adjective that appears

before the word it modifies.

well-to-do individual	solid-state circuit
no-nonsense attitude	state-of-the-art computer
starry-eyed dreamer	user-friendly software

The team has out-of-date equipment.

But do not use hyphens if a compound adjective *follows* the word it modifies.

The team's equipment is out of date.

Do not hyphenate adverbs ending in *-ly* when they are combined with an adjective or participle.

Wrong: nearly-indestructible nylon, environmentally-friendly laws

Right: nearly indestructible nylon, environmentally friendly laws

Hyphenate the following:

✓ Fractions

two-thirds   four-fifths

✓ Compound numbers from twenty-one to ninety-nine

fifty-one   ninety-nine

✓ The combination of a number and a word

12-inch ruler   30-day month   10-cent coin

Use hyphens to divide words when they don't fit at the end of a line.

Word processors do a good job of dividing words at the right-hand margin. However, computers occasionally make mistakes, and you may not always be using a computer, so it's smart to know a few rules.

In general, put the hyphen between syllables or doubled letters.

put-ting   con-junc-tion   time-line

MY computer never makes mistakes . . .

If you don't know how to break a word into syllables, look up the word in a dictionary.

Don't divide one-syllable words.

thought   burned   noise

Don't divide a word if it creates a misleading pronunciation.

dancing, *not* danc-ing   hoping, *not* hop-ing

Don't divide the last word of a paragraph or page.

Parentheses   ( )

Parentheses create the effect of an aside, as if you were trying to say the words behind your hand. Use them only now and then, or your writing will lack directness.

Use parentheses to set off an explanation or to add information.

> The teacher (who chose not to reveal his identity) submitted a list of the crazy excuses he'd received to explain late homework.

When the parentheses contain a complete statement or question, put the closing punctuation mark inside the parentheses.

> (She is the shortstop.)

> (Was he dreaming?)

Period   .

Periods are useful at the ends of sentences and abbreviations. In England, the period is called a "full stop," which is a good description of what it does.

Use a period as follows:

✓ At the end of a declarative sentence (a statement)

> You can't hide a piece of broccoli in a glass of milk.

✓ At the end of an imperative sentence (instructions, requests, orders)

> Don't pick on your sister when she's holding a baseball bat.

✓ With some abbreviations and initials

> P.M.   Mr.   Ms.   Mrs.   vs.   etc.
> J. F. Kennedy, *but* JFK (no periods)

If an abbreviation ends a sentence, don't add a second period.

> We will expect you at 10 a.m.

An ellipsis is three evenly spaced periods. Use an ellipsis to indicate where something has been left out of quoted material.

> *"Consider the postage stamp. Its usefulness consists of its ability to stick to one thing. . .until it gets there."*
> —Anonymous

If the omission is between sentences, put the ellipsis after the period at the end of the first sentence.

> *Tomorrow is the most important thing in life . . . . It hopes we've learned something from yesterday.*
> —John Wayne

Question Mark ?

Put a question mark after a direct question (in other words, at the end of an interrogative sentence).

> Did you check out the website?
> Who is coming to the party?

Do not use a question mark with an indirect question or polite request.

Can I come?

> He asked who is coming to the party.
> Will you please close the door as you leave.

Quotation Marks   " "

Direct quotations are the exact words that someone says. Indirect quotations are what someone says expressed in slightly different words.

Use quotation marks to show a direct quotation.

Put only the words someone actually said inside the quotation marks.

> Samuel Johnson said, "A fishing rod is a stick with a hook at one end and a fool at the other."

Do not use quotation marks for an indirect quotation. The following example begins with an indirect quotation and ends with a direct quotation:

> *My mom said she learned how to swim when someone took her out in the lake and threw her off the boat. I said, "Mom, they weren't trying to teach you how to swim."*
>
> —Paula Poundstone

Put quotation marks around titles of songs, short stories, poems, and parts of whole publications, such as articles in magazines or encyclopedias.

> "The Star-Spangled Banner"   "Auld Lang Syne"

> John Steinbeck's "The Red Pony" is required reading.

If you have a computer, use **italics** for titles of movies, television and radio series, plays, books, magazines, and newspapers.

> *New York Times   National Geographic   Titanic*

> *Harry Potter and the Sorcerer's Stone   X-Files*

If you are writing by hand, **underline** titles of movies, books, magazines, and similar major works. Put quotation marks around titles of shorter works (stories, articles, poems).

> I read a <u>National Geographic</u> article titled "Valley of the Mummies".

Punctuate quoted material as follows:

✓ Put commas and periods *inside* the quotation marks.

> "xxxxxx,"   "xxxxxxx."

✓ Place all other punctuation marks *outside* the quotation marks, unless they are part of a title or the material that is being quoted.

> Can you believe he said "No"?
> As she stomped out of the room, she shouted, "No!"
> When your dad is mad and asks, "Do I look stupid?" don't answer.
> Have you heard the poem "Twinkle Twinkle Little Aardvark"?

Semicolon ;

The semicolon provides a stronger break than a comma does, but a weaker one than a period.

Use a semicolon between closely related independent clauses when they are not joined by *and*.

Copy from one, it's plagiarism; copy from two, it's research.

—Wilson Mizner

She got her good looks from her father; he's a plastic surgeon.

—Groucho Marx

Use a semicolon to separate a series of items that contain commas.

The students tried out for the roles of Babyface Dillon, the villain; Sam Spade, the clever detective; and Dixie Darling, Sam's sweetheart.

5

What You Need to Know about Spelling and Capitalization

● ●

Spelling

There are two big reasons to be a good speller. (1) It helps get your ideas across; misspelled words can mislead or confuse someone trying to read what you've written. (2) Misspelled words make you look careless and sloppy. Put the other way around, correct spelling makes you look good.

Please don't assume that a spell-checker takes care of spelling for you. A spell-checker helps find *most* misspelled words in what you've written on your computer. But as you may have discovered already, the spell-checker doesn't catch every mistake. As long as you use real words, the spell-checker is happy; for example, it wouldn't notice any misspelled words in the following sentence:

> **Wrong:** Witch won of you're feat is soar?
> **Right:** Which one of your feet is sore?

Spell-checkers *will* catch an error such as "acrost," but if you have trouble with spelling, you might want to have someone who's a good speller look over your homework before you turn it in.

The most enjoyable way to improve spelling is to read good books. As you read, notice how the words look. This helps you learn when a word "looks right."

Can you spell supercalifragilisticexpialidocious?

Also important is looking up unfamiliar words in a dictionary. Roam around the pages while you're there. Consider the dictionary a good way to get acquainted with our rich language.

The examples in the following pages will help you understand some spelling rules. Once you're familiar with a few of them, you'll be on your way to being a good speller.

Making Nouns Plural

The usual way to make a noun plural is to add *s*.

shoe/shoes   hat/hats   town/towns

But if a noun ends in *s, x, ch, sh,*
or *z,* you should add *es*.

boxes   bushes
beaches   waltzes
messes

There are more rules about
making nouns plural, so tighten
your seatbelts. Here goes!

If the noun ends in *o*

✓ When a **vowel** comes before the *o,* you always add **only** *s*.

> rodeo/rodeos   studio/studios
> kangaroo/kangaroos   zoo/zoos

✓ When a **consonant** comes before the *o,* you **usually** add *es*.

> potato/potatoes   torpedo/torpedoes
> mosquito/mosquitoes   hero/heroes

✓ When the noun ending in *o* is a musical term, you add **only** *s*.

> solo/solos   piano/pianos   banjo/banjos

Exceptions: *zeros, avocados, mementos,* plus about forty more. A
dictionary is a good place to find out how to spell the plural of a
word. If no plural is listed, it means the plural is formed by
adding *s* or *es*.

If the noun ends in *y*

✓ When a **consonant** comes before the *y*, change the *y* to *i* and add *es*.

company/companies   study/studies
country/countries   celebrity/celebrities

✓ When a **vowel** comes before the *y*, just add *s*.

monkey/monkeys   attorney/attorneys   buoy/buoys
donkey/donkeys   bluejay/bluejays   cowboy/cowboys

If the noun ends in *f* or *fe*, change the *f* to *v* and add *es*.

loaf/loaves   knife/knives   life/lives

Exceptions: chef/chefs   chief/chiefs

With numbers, letters, and acronyms

(An acronym is a word made up of the first letters of a group of words: for example, MVP = **M**ost **V**aluable **P**layer.)

✓ Add *s* to form plurals.

the late 1990s   the three Rs
in twos and threes   MVPs

✓ Add *'s* to abbreviations that have periods, to lowercase letters, and to words if needed to avoid cofusion.

Be sure to dot all your i's and cross all your t's.
Mind your p's and q's.
My math and science teachers both have Ph.D.'s.

Adding Suffixes

Remember? A suffix is a word part (for example, *-hood, -ing, -less*) that we add to the *end* of a root word (*child, color, thought*) to make a new word (*childhood, coloring, thoughtless*).

When adding a suffix that begins with a vowel, double the final consonant of the root word in the following cases:

✓ The root word ends in a single consonant with a single vowel in front of it.

> swim/swimming   grin/grinning   flap/flapper
> god/goddess   put/putting   regret/regrettable

✓ The root word is a one-syllable word or is accented on the last syllable.

> zip/zipped   bag/baggage   prefer/preferred
> occur/occurrence   transfer/transferred   commit/committed

But the rules change when the root word ends in a silent *e*.

✓ If the suffix begins with a consonant, do not drop the silent *e* at the end of the root word.

> care/careless   like/likeness   state/statement

✓ If the suffix begins with a vowel, drop the silent e at the end of the root word.

> move/movable   use/usage   age/aging   value/valuable
> force/forcible   like/likable   state/stating   shine/shining

Exceptions: *mileage, hoeing,* and words such as *manageable* or *serviceable,* where dropping the final *e* would change the last consonant from a soft sound to a hard sound.

Words with *ei* or *ie*

Maybe you've already learned the jingle that helps you with these words:

> Put i before e,
> except after c.

So far, so good. The "*i* before *e*" part covers words such as *piece, brief,* and *niece;* the "except after *c*" part covers words like *receive, ceiling,* and *deceive.* But then there are the exceptions. When a syllable is pronounced *a,* as in *neighbor* or *weigh,* the word is *usually* spelled *ei.* And on and on.

You may want to memorize the spelling of a few common *ei/ie* words. Here's a sentence that includes many of the **exceptions** to the "*i* before *e,* except after *c*" rule:

> In a **weird** moment of **leisure,** they **seized** a **species** of **financier** they hoped would be **either** rich or smart; it was **neither**.

Words with Unsounded Letters

Some words have letters that are not pronounced, such as the *b* in *lamb* and *debt.* It's probably a good idea to memorize these "spelling demons." Here's a short list to start you on your way.

Silent c:	muscle
Silent g:	gnarled, campaign, sign, light
Silent h:	rhythm, khaki, exhaust, exhibit
Silent k:	knew, knife
Silent l:	could, should, would, half
Silent p:	pneumonia, receipt, corps

Silent s:	aisle, island, corps, chassis
Silent t:	often, soften, mortgage
Silent w:	write, wrong, answer, two, who, whose, whole

ACTUALLY, THESE SPELLING DEMONS AREN'T SO BAD ONCE YOU GET TO KNOW THEM!

Capitalization

Capital letters are a guide for the reader. We capitalize the first word of a sentence to tell readers, Hello—this is where the sentence begins! And we capitalize a proper noun to let readers know it's the name of a specific person or place. In general, you should capitalize proper nouns, certain words in titles and quotations, and words you want to emphasize.

Some people write with all capital letters to avoid having to decide which words to capitalize. Bad idea! Writing that's all in capital letters is hard to read. Furthermore, since capital letters make a word stand out, if you write with all caps, nothing stands out.

Which of the following gets the idea across better?

      I SAID, "NO!"   *or*   I said, "NO!"

Reserve capitals for emphasis and for the uses that follow.

First Letters

Capitalize the following:

✓ The first word of a sentence

Kitesurfing is a new extreme sport.

✓ The first word following a colon if it begins a complete sentence

There's one way to find out if a man is honest: Ask him. If he says yes, you know he is crooked.
—Mark Twain

✓ The first word of a quotation

Laughter is the shortest distance between two people.
—Victor Borge

✓ If the quotation is interrupted, the second part is capitalized only if it begins a new sentence.

> *"Take some more tea," the March Hare said to Alice, very earnestly.*
> *"I've had nothing yet," Alice replied in an offended tone, "so I can't take more."*
> *"You mean you can't take less," said the Hatter. "It's very easy to take more than nothing."*
>
> —Lewis Carroll

Titles

✓ In titles of books, plays, television programs, songs, and movies, capitalize the first and last words, plus all important words.

> **Book:** *Julie of the Wolves*
> **Song:** "After the Gold Rush"
> **TV Series:** *Party of Five*

✓ Do not capitalize articles, conjunctions, or the word *to* when it's part of an infinitive.

> *Buffy the Vampire Slayer*
> *Stop the World, I Want to Get Off!*

✓ Capitalize personal titles only if they come before the name and are not separated by a comma.

> *the president, Abraham Lincoln, . . .*
> *President Abraham Lincoln*

Names and Proper Nouns

the Astrodome	the Big Apple
John Doe	New Orleans
Alexander the Great	*Roe v. Wade*
the Middle East	General Motors
the Amazon River	World Wildlife Federation
U.S. Treasury Dept.	Library of Congress

Do not capitalize words such as *government, federal, administration,* or *agency* unless they are part of a specific name.

> The Federal Emergency Management Agency offers government loans to flood victims.

✓ Capitalize the kinship name of a relative when it comes before a proper name.

> Aunt Tillie   Cousin Ezekiel   Grandma Moses

✓ Do not capitalize a relative's name when it **follows** an article (*a, an,* or *the*).

> the father of the pilot

✓ or a possessive pronoun (such as *my* or *their*).

> my sister
>
> He spoke to his uncle. Uncle Joe didn't answer.

Compass Points and Regional Terms

✓ Capitalize compass points and regions when they refer to specific geographic areas or are part of a title.

> the West, Midwest, South   the Southern Hemisphere
> Chicago's South Side   Southeast Asia

✓ Do not capitalize words that merely suggest direction or position.

> western Texas   northern lights
> central time zone   south of the border

Calendar

✓ Capitalize days of the week, months, and holidays.

> Thursday   Fourth of July   Halloween   August

✓ Do not capitalize the seasons.

> summer solstice   spring equinox
>
> We have to change our clocks in spring and fall.

6

Some Tricky Words You Need to Know

●●●●●●●●●●●●●●●●●●●●●●●●

WRITE OR RIGHT?

USE HEIGHTH!

Power Tools

Words are your tools. The more words you know, the more tools you have, and the more powerful your writing will be.

If words are going to work for you, you need to know more than how to spell them. You need to know how to use them correctly in sentences. The tricky words in the lists that follow are often used incorrectly or confused with other words.

I've included some "nonwords" in the list. These are words such as *acrost* that have a correct word buried somewhere inside, waiting to be liberated. This list will help you find them and turn them into useful words.

I've also included a list of homonyms. Homonyms are two or more words that have the same pronunciation but different spellings and meanings. *There, their,* and *they're* are homonyms. The list will help you make sure you've chosen the right one.

Use these lists to add words to your everyday vocabulary. They will help make you a writing powerhouse!

The difference between the right word and the almost right word is really a large matter—it's the difference between lightning and the lightning bug.

—Mark Twain

Tricky Words

Where appropriate, the following abbreviations for parts of speech are used: *n.* = *noun;* *v.* = *verb;* *adj.* = *adjective;* *adv.* = *adverb;* *conj.* = *conjunction;* *prep.* = *preposition.*

Accept: *v.,* to take what is given
Except: *prep.,* but; other than
Use an objective pronoun with *except* (*me, her, him, them*). See page 35.

> Everyone was there to **accept** their awards **except** me.

Acrost: a nonword; use *across*

Advice: *n.,* suggestion; opinion about a course of action
Advise: *v.,* to give advice; to suggest or inform

> I **advise** you to take her **advice**.

Affect: *v.,* to influence; to have an effect on
Effect: *n.,* result; consequence

> The **effect** of his weird story was clear; it **affected** the jury's "not guilty" decision.

Alot: a nonword; should be two words: *a lot*

Among: *prep.,* Use when referring to three or more people or things.

> **among** the three of us

Between: *prep.,* Use when referring to two people or things.

> **between** you and me

Angel: *n.,* an immortal heavenly being; a wonderful person
Angle: *n.,* a mathematical term; a devious scheme

> Be an **angel** and figure out the **angle** of this intersection for me.

Anxious: *adj.,* uneasy; worried
Eager: *adj.,* strongly desiring something

> They were **eager** to go to Magic Mountain, but felt **anxious** about the long lines.

Bad: An **adjective** meaning poor or inferior; *bad* is the right word to use with linking verbs, such as *feel* or *look*.

> I feel **bad**.

Badly: An **adverb** meaning in a bad manner.

> I feel **bad** that I played so **badly** during the match.

Don't say "I feel badly" unless you mean that you have a poor sense of touch.

Bring: Use this verb to indicate movement *toward* the speaker.

> **Bring** the book to me.

Take: Use this verb to indicate movement *away from* the speaker.

> **Take** this form to the principal's office. (*Not* Bring this form to the principal's office.)

What did I do?

Can: *v.,* able or having the power to do something

> She **can** do 100 push-ups.

May: *v.,* having permission to do something

> You **may** leave the table.

Coma: state of deep unconsciousness
Comma: a punctuation mark

Conscience: *n.,* ability to know right from wrong
Conscious: *adj.,* awake; aware of one's environment

> I was **conscious** of the nagging voice of my **conscience**.

Convince: *v.,* to bring to belief by reason or argument
Persuade: *v.,* This verb has the same meaning as *convince,* but *persuade* is the right word to use when an action is suggested: *convince* **that,** *persuade* **to.**

> She **convinced** me **that** the Earth is flat.
> He **persuaded** me **to join** the Flat Earth Society.

Desert: *n.,* a hot, dry region
Dessert: *n.,* final course of
a meal, usually sweet

Different From/Different Than: Both mean unlike, not similar. But *different from* is the better choice if what follows is a single noun or pronoun.

> Her tattoo is **different from** mine.

Use *different than* when what follows is a clause.

> Having a tattoo today is **different than** when I was a kid.

Disburse: *v.,* to pay out
Disperse: *v.,* to scatter

> The crowd **dispersed** after the money was **disbursed**.

Drownded: a nonword; use *drowned*

Ecology: *n.,* study of the relationship of organisms and their environment; not a synonym for environment
Environment: *n.,* surroundings

Emigrate: *v.,* to leave one country in order to settle in another (You emigrate *from* a country.)

> My grandparents **emigrated** from Italy.

Immigrate: *v.,* to enter and settle permanently in a foreign country (You immigrate *to* a country.)

> They plan to **immigrate** to Israel.

Enthused: Avoid this word. Use *enthusiastic* or find another way to express the idea.

Excape: a nonword; use *escape*

Farther: *adv.,* to a greater distance
Further: *adj.,* more; additional

Use *farther* when physical distance is involved; use *further* when you mean "to a greater extent."

> Today I flew my stunt kite **farther** than ever.
> Kitesurfing is **further** evidence that some people like dangerous sports.

Female: not a synonym for *woman* or *girl* (Write *a group of women,* not *a group of females.*)

Fewer: *adj.,* a smaller number; use with things that can be counted (fewer telescopes).

Less: *adj.,* not so much; use with things that can't be counted (less noise, less mystery).

> **fewer** assignments, **less** homework
> **fewer** jobs, **less** pay

Heighth: a nonword; use *height*

Home in: *v.,* to proceed toward an objective

> After a series of failures, the researchers finally **homed in** on a cure for the common cold.

Hone: *v.,* to sharpen

> The team **honed** its debating skills.

Don't write about "honing in" on anything; the word to use with *in* is *home* (home in).

Irregardless: a nonword; use *regardless*

Kind: *singular adj.,* Write *that kind* or *those kinds,* not *those kind*.

Later: *adv.,* after the usual or expected time

> Because his alarm didn't work, he arrived **later** than the others did.

Latter: *adj.,* the second of two just mentioned

> Wilhelmina and Gertrude are best friends; the **latter** is also a good friend of mine.

Lay: *v.,* to place or put down; requires a direct object (See page 10–11.)

> **Lay** your cards on the table.

Lay and *laid* are also forms of the past tense of the verb *lie*.

> The room stopped spinning when I **lay** down.
> She **laid** the newspaper on the counter.

Lie: *v.,* to recline; to assume a horizontal position; never has a direct object

> **Lie** on the grass and gaze at the stars.

Learn: *v.,* to gain knowledge through study or experience; not a synonym for *teach*

> I **taught** her how to fly a kite. (*Not* I learned her how to fly a kite.)

Leave: not a synonym for *let*

> **Let** go of the rattlesnake.
> (*Not* Leave go of the rattlesnake.)

OKAY, BUT SHE HAS TO LET GO FIRST!

RATTLE RATTLE

Lend: a verb that means to give someone the temporary use of something (Careful writers write *Lend me your pencil* instead of *Loan me your pencil.*)

Loan: a noun that refers to the temporary use of something

> I needed a **loan** to buy my car.

Like: *prep.,* similar to (Use before nouns or pronouns.)

> He sings **like** Elvis.

This is one of our most overused words. Try removing it from your vocabulary!

As: *adv.,* equally; in the same manner (Use with phrases.)

> Do **as** I say, not **as** I do.

Loose: *adj.,* not fastened
Lose: *v.,* opposite of *win* and *find*

Media: *n.,* more than one means of mass communication, such as television and newspapers; a plural word requiring a plural verb (The singular of *media* is *medium*.)

> The **media** were present with dozens of reporters and cameras.

Moral: *adj.,* relating to good behavior or character; *n.,* the lesson taught by a story

> My little brothers won't let me read aloud the **morals** at the end of Aesop's fables. Will this affect their **moral** development?

Morale: *n.,* the spirit of an individual or group

> Workers do a better job when **morale** is high.

Of: not a substitute for *have* when used with words such as *could, should,* and *would; could have* or *could've,* **not** *could of*

> **Wrong:** I would **of** come sooner, but Scooter hid my sneakers.
> **Right:** I would **have** come sooner, but Scooter hid my sneakers.

Persecute: *v.,* to harass persistently; to give someone a hard time

Prosecute: *v.,* to bring someone before a court of law

> If you don't stop **persecuting** me, I'll get the district attorney to **prosecute** you for being a bully.

Predominant: *adj.,* most common; having the greatest influence

> The **predominant** color was blue.

Predominate: *v.,* to be of greater power, importance, or quantity

> Of all the colors, blue **predominated.**

Probaly: a nonword; use *probably*

Reconize: a nonword; use *recognize*

Respectfully: *adv.,* full of respect (*I respectfully disagree.*); sometimes used in the formal closing of a letter (*Respectfully yours*)

Respectively: *adv.,* individually; in the order given

> Naomi and Patrick played the parts of Titania and Puck, **respectively**. (In other words, Naomi was Titania and Patrick was Puck.)

Do not sign a letter *Respectively yours.*

Set: *v.,* to put in a specific place

Sit: *v.,* to assume an upright position with the weight on the buttocks

> **Sit** here while I **set** down my package.

Snuck: an informal past tense and past participle of the verb *to sneak* (The correct past tense of *sneak* is *sneaked*.)

Somewheres: a nonword; instead, use *somewhere* (This is also true for *anywheres* and *nowheres;* write *anywhere* and *nowhere*.)

Stanch: *v.,* to stop the flow
Staunch: *adj.,* loyal; steadfast

> If you are wounded, you might wish for a **staunch** friend to **stanch** the flow of blood.

Suspect: *v.,* to regard as probable

> I **suspect** that they are guilty.

Suspicion: *n.,* hint; the act of suspecting something

> I have a **suspicion** that they are guilty. (*not* I suspicion that they are guilty.)

Than: *conj.,* compared with
Then: *adv.,* next in time, space, or order

> Stuart **then** said, "I'm taller **than** you are."

Theirselves: a nonword; use *themselves*

Umpire: *n.,* someone appointed to rule on plays in various sports
Empire: *n.,* a group of territories under one government

> Within the British **Empire**, more than a dozen sports require **umpires**.

Way: *singular n.,* a singular word when describing distance (Write a **long** *way* **to go**, *not* **a long** *ways* to go.)

Homonyms

Allowed: *v.,* permitted
Aloud: *adv.,* out loud; with the voice

> Reading **aloud** is not **allowed** in this room.

Capital: *n.,* wealth; the city that is the seat of government; an uppercase letter
Capitol: *n.,* the building in which state or federal officials meet (When referring to the home of the U.S. Congress, *Capitol* is always capitalized.)

> People who work in the **Capitol** disburse a great deal of the taxpayers' **capital**.

Complement: *v.,* to complete a whole or satisfy a need
Compliment: *v.,* to praise; *n.,* praise

> She **complimented** him on how well the apple pie **complemented** the rest of the meal he had cooked.

Discreet: *adj.,* showing good judgment in behavior or attitude
Discrete: *adj.,* separate; individually distinct

Principal: *n.,* head of a school or company

> She has been **principal** of the school for less than a year.

> *n.,* money that earns interest
> The **principal** in the account is earning 5 percent interest.

> *adj.,* main; chief
> The **principal** investigator is named Dick Tracy.

Principle: *n.,* rule; standard

> The **principle** Be Prepared is a Boy Scout tradition.

Role: *n.,* a part in a play
Roll: *n.,* a list of names; a small rounded portion of bread; *v.,* to move by turning over and over

> In his **role** as rodeo star, he had to hold on when the steer **rolled** over on him.

Stationary: *adj.,* not moving; fixed in position
Stationery: *n.,* writing paper and envelopes

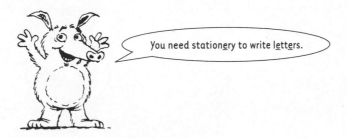

You need stationery to write letters.

Suite: *n.,* a series of connecting rooms
Sweet: *adj.,* having a sugary or pleasing taste

Their: possessive pronoun meaning "belonging to them"
There: *adv.,* at that place
They're: contraction of "they are"

> **They're** flying **their** kites **there**.

Write: *v.,* to use an implement such as pencil or keyboard to put letters and words on paper or computer screen
Right: *adj.,* in a correct manner

WHAT THIS BOOK HELPS YOU DO!

7

What You Need to Know about Organization

Putting the Parts Together

To assemble a bicycle, you need a complete set of parts. Then you have to put the parts together in a certain order. For example, you can't install the spokes after the tires have been put on. If you put it together right, the bike will take you from one place to another without falling apart.

In writing, the "parts" are words, sentences, and paragraphs. So far in this book, you've been working on those parts. In this chapter, you'll learn how to put them together. What you write will take your readers from one place to another, too. That's communication!

Get Started

The first step is choosing a topic. Whether your subject is lasers, the problem of child labor, or your dog Scooter, if you pick a subject that interests you, you improve the odds that readers will find it interesting, too.

At the start, many people find that a blank piece of paper or computer screen stops them in their tracks. The best way around the problem is to brainstorm. Let's go through the process, step-by-step.

Jot down or type out the ideas, examples, descriptions, and details you want to include. Put them all into words. Don't worry about the order yet—just write. If it helps you get started, answer the five Ws: who? what? when? where? and why?

Take the story about Scooter. What do you want readers to know about him? Make a list of possible ideas or topics.

✓ How you got him
✓ What breed of dog he is
✓ What he looks like
✓ His personality quirks
✓ Funny things he does

How about a story about a pet aardvark?

✓ Trouble he's been in
✓ What makes him different from other dogs

If your subject is lasers, your "dump" of ideas might look like this.

✓ How they work
✓ Inventors
✓ Different uses
✓ Benefits

If the subject is child labor, topics might include the nature of the problem, people and organizations working to change it, and what an individual can do.

What do you know about your subject? What can you find out about it from books and the Internet? Write it down.

Have a Plan

Next, start organizing your ideas. Do some topics look like main ideas? Do others look like supporting details? Which should come first? How do they fit together? What examples or anecdotes illustrate your points?

If you're writing with pencil and paper, draw a big balloon in which to contain each main idea. Put the supporting details inside smaller balloons, and connect them to the appropriate big balloon.

If you're writing on a computer, type each main idea as a heading. Type the supporting details under the appropriate heading.

Now, put your balloons or lists into a logical order. Think of yourself as a guide who's showing the readers a trail map and saying, "We are here, this is where we're going, and here's what we'll see along the way." Number the balloons or lists in the order you want to present them.

Your writing needs a beginning (where you introduce your topic), a middle (where you develop the topic with more information and more details), and an end (where you summarize and present your closing thoughts).

Within that loose framework, you have choices about how to organize the paragraphs. If you want to tell Scooter's story in the order in which things happened; that's called **chronological order**. Start with how and when you got Scooter, what he was like as a puppy (chewing on sneakers, digging holes to bury bones), adventures you had as he was growing up (the time he

THE CURIOUS LIFE OF SCOOTER

He was an unusual puppy from the first day he showed up on our doorstep.

As the neighborhood peacemaker, he settles everyone's disputes.

It's the same schedule every day.

Yoga from 2 to 4 o'clock.

(Don't interrupt!)

Then it's banjo practice until 5:30.

At night Scooter retires to his room to write his autobiography.

I hope he mentions me!

helped you find your way home), and what he's like now. Close by describing what having Scooter means to you or what you like best about him.

There are other ways to organize a composition.

✓ Comparison and contrast: comparing things that are alike in important ways (sometimes called **analogy**), and pointing out ways they are different (**contrast**)

✓ Steps in a process (describing how something works)

✓ Order of importance (first presenting less important details, and then more important ones—or vice versa)

You could combine the last two ways to organize your material (steps in a process and order of importance) when you write about the subject of lasers. A topic outline might look like this.

Opening
- What is a laser? How does it work?
- What does the acronym LASER stand for? (<u>L</u>ight <u>A</u>mplification by <u>S</u>timulated <u>E</u>mission of <u>R</u>adiation)

Middle
- Who invented it? When? Where?
- How are lasers used?
  - to make CDs
  - as land-surveying equipment
  - during surgery
  - to correct vision
  - in lumber mills (to saw logs efficiently)
  - during research
  - to study combustion

Absolutely <u>A</u>wesome, <u>R</u>ad <u>D</u>ude, <u>V</u>ery <u>A</u>ble, <u>R</u>ugged, and <u>K</u>nowledgeable

Ending
- Importance of lasers in our lives
- Conclusions about the range of ways we use lasers
  - from guided missiles to restoring eyesight

When you've settled on your approach to presenting the material, it's time to start writing paragraphs.

Write It Up

Number the lists or balloons in the order you want to create your "trail map," and then write: only one topic for each paragraph. Make one sentence your **topic sentence**; in it, tell readers what the paragraph is about. The topic sentence is often the first one in the paragraph, but it may appear at the end as a summarizing statement.

The other sentences in the paragraph develop the idea presented in the topic sentence with related facts, examples, or supporting detail. When you introduce a new idea or topic, start a new paragraph. Be sure to show it's a new paragraph by indenting the first line of each paragraph or by putting an extra space between paragraphs.

A Model Paragraph

Let's look at a paragraph written by the Canadian author Farley Mowat. He describes his dog Mutt's appearance and how it helps Mutt when he's chasing a gopher or cat.

> If he was unique in attitude, he was also unique in his appearance. . . . His hindquarters were elevated several inches higher than his forequarters; and at the same time he was distinctly canted from left to right. The result was that, when he was approaching, he appeared to be drifting off about three points to starboard, while simultaneously giving an eerie impression of a submarine starting on a crash dive. It was impossible to tell . . . exactly where he was heading. . . . His eyes gave no clue, for they were so close-set that he looked to be . . . somewhat cross-eyed. The total illusion had its practical advantages, for gophers and cats pursued by Mutt could seldom decide where he was aiming until they discovered, too late, that he was actually on a collision course with them.

The Dog Who Wouldn't Be, by Farley Mowat. Boston: Little Brown and Company, 1957.

Notice how Mowat organizes his paragraph. His topic is Mutt's appearance, and his topic sentence is "If he was unique in attitude, he was also unique in his appearance." The other sentences in the paragraph provide detail and examples that illustrate just how unique Mutt's appearance is.

Topic: Mutt's Appearance

- Description of hind- and forequarters (comparison with submarine)
- Description of eyes
- Practical advantages of Mutt's appearance

Your paragraph should have a unified feeling, like Mowat's. Make every sentence relate to the main idea.

Paragraph Length

How long should paragraphs be? They can be as short as one sentence. You use one- or two-sentence paragraphs to make important parts stand out. But this doesn't work if you do it too often. When you use a lot of short paragraphs, none of them stand out—they're just monotonous.

On the other hand, paragraphs that are too long look like fortresses. They are hard to read, and people might just skip over them. When you have a lot to say about a topic, break it up into separate paragraphs.

Mowat does this with Mutt's appearance. He has more to say about it, but he knows his readers need some breathing space. So he begins a new paragraph with the reminder that he's still talking about how Mutt looks. Mowat uses some fancy words in this paragraph, but if you read it carefully, I think you'll get the idea. And there's always a dictionary!

An even more disquieting physical characteristic was the fact that his hind legs moved at a slower speed than did his front ones. This was theoretically explicable on the grounds that his hind legs were much longer than his forelegs—but an understanding of this explanation could not dispel the unsettling impression that Mutt's forward section was slowly and relentlessly pulling away from the tardy after-end.

The picture of Mutt's front legs slowly pulling away from the rest of him makes me smile every time I read it.

Connecting the Paragraphs

When your organization is logical, readers won't feel yanked around or confused. You also help readers follow your line of thought if you link paragraphs with "connecting words" such as *also* and *however*. Such words let readers know what's coming.

Say you're writing a book report. In one paragraph, you describe how the author made you laugh; in the next paragraph, you write about parts of the story that made you sad. Warn readers of the contrast by starting your new paragraph with connecting words such as *even though* or *but*.

If your paragraphs describe a certain order of events, begin each paragraph with words that signal the order: *first, next, finally*.

Here are some examples of connecting words and where to use them.

Connecting Words	To Show
also, what's more, again, furthermore, in addition	More of the same is coming
first, second, next, then, finally, last	Order of events, sequence in time
on the other hand, but, in contrast, however, nonetheless, even though, instead, although	Change of direction, contrary or different view
because, since, as a result	Cause and effect
thus, therefore, as you can see, finally	Conclusion, summary

Titles

As you're writing your essay, think about what would be a good title. The title is the first thing readers see. Use it as an opportunity to the hook them.

Here are some title ideas for the subjects I've suggested.

Lasers in Our Lives

Where in the World Are Children Working?

Scooter: A Dog's Life

Samples

Now let's look at how you might organize several different kinds of writing.

Narrative or Biographical Sketch

Write about one of your relatives. Maybe your grandparents would tell you what life was like when they were your age. Make a list of questions to ask them—I guarantee they'll be interested in answering them! You could write about someone famous or about your best friend, or choose to write about the person you know best: yourself!

- What it was like when you were little
  - your earliest memories
- What your family is like: parents, sisters, brothers, aunts, uncles, cousins, special family friends
- Your favorite things to do
  - play computer games   - play soccer
  - read   - camp
- What's important to you

Use vivid details to bring yourself to life, as Mowat brings Mutt to life.

Book Report

A good way to organize a book report is to ask yourself a lot of questions about the book, and then put your answers into a logical sequence.

Questions to ask

- What is the book about? What's the theme? Maybe it's about growing up or what happens when parents divorce. Does the author stick with the theme? Does the author show you something about the theme that you hadn't thought of? What happens in the story? Be brief.

- What do you know about the author's life? other books?

- Why do you think the author wrote the book?

- Does the author's writing style work? Are the scary parts actually scary? Give an example.
  Do the funny parts make you laugh? Provide an example.
  Are the characters believable? Which was your favorite?

- How does the book compare with other books you've read? Better, worse . . .

I threw it on the floor!

- How did the book make you feel?
  What important things did you get from reading the book?
  Were you glad you read it?

Answering questions like these, rather than just retelling the book's plot or theme, will help you write a better report.

Thank-You Letter

Writing a thank-you note is a great idea when someone has done something nice for you. If you received a gift, you could describe what you like about it and how you've used it. Is there any family news or news of special things going on at school you should include? Remember to say Thank You!

(Date)

Dear Grandma and Grandpa,

Thanks for the great book you gave me for my birthday. I guess Dad told you how I've started making my own kites, and *Chinese Artistic Kites* gives me lots of good ideas. I never knew there were so many ways to make kites!

Next time you're here, I'll show you what I've made. In the meantime, maybe I can get someone to take a picture of me flying my new asterisk-frame rigid-wing kite (when it's built!). When you see what it looks like, maybe you can help me think of a really cool name for it.

Thanks again for the book.

Love,

Dylan

Persuasive Essay

Suppose you want to raise money for your school band. An important part of such a campaign would be writing letters to the school board or the county board of supervisors. You could also get results by sending editorials to a website or to the local newspaper. (They call these Op Ed pieces, which is short for "opinion editorial pieces.")

You might organize your letter or editorial about the school band along these lines.

- State the problem
  - There's not enough money for instruments.
  - There's no transportation to school games, where the band could play.
- Explain why having a band matters
  - Students learn to work together.
  - It gives students an incentive to practice and perform for live audiences.
- List the benefits
  - Music adds to the total school experience.
  - The band develops school spirit.
  - Music develops the individual.

Music soothes the savage aardvark.

Or suppose you want to convince the city council in your town that the municipal park is out-of-date. The students in Anoka, Minnesota, did just that. They successfully proposed that the city redesign the municipal park and turn a long-neglected amphitheater into a place to hold concerts and perform plays.

I don't know exactly what they wrote to the city council, but a letter about the park might have looked something like this.

Dear City Council Members:

We are a group of students at Anoka Middle School who have noticed that our municipal park is badly run-down and out-of-date. The playground doesn't have any of the high-tech equipment that is available now, and some of the equipment is so worn out that it's even dangerous.

A municipal pool and a place for skateboarding would be great additions to the park. When kids have neat places like that to go to, they don't get into as much trouble.

How about having a day-care center and a senior center? Maybe they could be combined!

Well, those are just a few of our ideas. We have a lot more, and we want to be part of making the park a place we will use. We are willing to help during every step: raising money (we have some ideas about that, too), designing the new park, and helping to build it.

We plan to present our proposal to the next city council meeting. If you would like to reach us in the meantime, you can call our teacher, _____, at XXX-XXXX.

Thank you.

Sincerely yours,

P.S. How about having a community vegetable patch? That's another place where seniors and kids can work together.

As I said, although that's not a letter the students actually wrote, it may be like ones they did send. Anoka students even managed to win funding from the World Bank for one of their projects, and you can't do that without putting some words on paper. Their World Bank project is an Infoline Café that enables them to exchange ideas on the Internet with students in Ecuador. As one of the students concluded, "If you put your heart and mind into something, you can succeed."

The story about Anoka is based on a press release provided by American News Service.

8

What You Need to Know about Writing Style

●●●●●●●●●●●●●●●●●●●●●●●●

Powerhouse Writing

The kind of style I'm talking about here has nothing to do with clothing or hair. It's the writing style that changes you from a ho-hum, ordinary writer to a standout one.

So far, I've told you how to write correctly. That's important. But your writing might still be uninteresting. Here are my special tips for keeping your readers awake instead of putting them to sleep.

Be Brief

People use too many words. They tend to just ramble on and on. In fact, wordiness may be the most common flaw in writing. To start on a diet of lean writing, look at the left-hand column in the list below. Do you see any words you use? If so, streamline them as suggested.

Wordy	Better
both alike	alike
first time ever	first time
for free	free
free gift	gift
the reason is because	the reason is
this here	this
unexpected surprise	surprise
various different	various **or** different
why this happened is	the reason is

Or how about sentences with extra words like these?

Wordy: The **age** of the puppy was six weeks **old** when we got him.
Better: The puppy was six weeks old when we got him.

Wordy: There are some students **who** need special P.E. classes.
Better: Some students need special P.E. classes.

Wordy: The **reason** I'm late is **because** I missed the bus.
Better: I'm late because I missed the bus.

I've heard *that* one before!

Readers appreciate it when you don't waste their time. Read what you write—again and again—looking for words to chop out.

Add the word *redundant* to your vocabulary. It's a dandy word that means "unnecessarily repetitious," like the wordy sentences in the examples.

Use the Active Voice

In the active voice, the subject of the sentence *is doing* something; in the passive voice, something *is being done to* the subject.

The passive voice tends to be wordy and indirect; it lacks the punch of the active voice.

Passive: The story was written by David.
Active: David wrote the story.

Here's an example where both passive and active voice are appropriate.

Poor: When the ballots were counted, the office of class president had been won by Carmen by a large margin.
Better: When the ballots were counted, Carmen had won a decisive victory as class president.

What's important about the ballots is their being counted, not who did the counting, so using the passive voice in that part of the sentence is suitable. But clearly changing to the active voice makes the rest of the sentence livelier.

Write with Variety

Nothing puts readers to sleep faster than the same kind of sentence, over and over.

> I like to skateboard. I have five skateboards. I can do ollies on my skateboard. I have one with a lot of stickers.

A series of clauses beginning with *and* is another way to bore readers. Don't get into such tedious ruts.

Boring: And then we went to a movie, and then we had a pizza, and then we went home.

Better: After the movie, we had a pizza and then went home.

To avoid monotony, make some sentences long and some short.

Short: Don't squat with spurs on.

Long: If you squat with spurs on, you will end up with a deeper understanding of a cowboy's life.

Use different beginnings for your sentences.

Open with a dependent clause.

> Until I learned how to skateboard, I was nobody.

Open with a preposition.

> With my new skateboard, I can do grinds.

Open with a participial phrase.

> Knowing how to do stalefishes has turned me into a skateboarding demon.

Join clauses in different ways.

> I have three skateboards, but the one I like best is a trick board.

The skateboard I like best is the one with the most stickers, even though it's the oldest one I have.

Be Consistent

If you start telling a story in your own voice (first person), using "I" and "we" to describe what's happening, tell the whole story that way.

If you start in the past tense, don't switch to the present tense in the middle of a sentence.

> **Poor:** I **was swimming** at the beach when suddenly I **see** a creature with sharp teeth and long tentacles coming my way.

> **Better:** I **was swimming** at the beach when suddenly I **saw** a creature with sharp teeth and long tentacles coming my way.

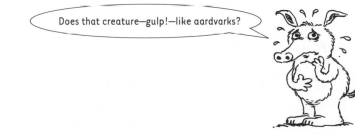

Does that creature—gulp!—like aardvarks?

Be Choosy about Words

Your basic writing tool is words. There are more than a million of them in the English language—that's more than in any other language! So you have plenty to choose from when you want to create a memorable picture in your reader's mind. The following suggestions will help turn you into a writing powerhouse.

Create Pictures with Your Words

Use words that appeal to the senses: words that help readers see or hear or touch something in their mind's eye. Describe the smell of cinnamon cookies baking, the feel of your cat's fur, the searing pain of burning your hand.

> **Vague:** Scooter is a good dog. He's always glad to see me.
> **Specific:** Scooter waits for me every afternoon at the corner. The way he wags his tail when he sees me, it's as if I'm the most important person in the world. Maybe I am.

Choose words that will create a vivid picture in your reader's mind. Use words like spaghetti and pineapple instead of "food." Write about confusion or envy or excitement, not just a "feeling."

> **Vague:** There was this creature coming after me.
> **Specific:** A slimy green creature with long tentacles and sharp teeth was coming after me.

Similes and metaphors help create pictures. A **simile** uses the word *like* to compare two unlike things.

> *Having a family is like having a bowling alley installed in your brain.*
>
> —Martin Mull

> Scooter's tail wags so fast, it's like a windshield wiper moving at warp speed.

A **metaphor** doesn't use the word *like* but instead says that something *is* something else. I create a metaphor if I write that similes and metaphors are powerful tools. I'm not saying they are *like* powerful tools, but that they *are* powerful tools.

Here's a sentence with both a simile and a metaphor.

Writing, like life itself, is a voyage of discovery.

—Henry Miller

Miller's simile uses the word *like* to compare life and writing; his metaphor compares writing and voyages by saying that life **is** a voyage.

Similes and metaphors add to your power as a writer.

Avoid Clichés and Slang

Writing with slang announces that you are sloppy and don't care about making a good impression. It's like arriving at the prom in a tank top and cutoffs. In writing, more formal "attire" is appropriate. I mean, go figure, like you know, slang really won't do!

The word *cliché* is pronounced "klee-shay"; it means "an over-worked expression," one that lacks originality. Writing with clichés tells readers you can't be bothered to put an idea in your own words; any tired phrase will do. Find fresher ways to express yourself than these.

as a matter of fact
basically
better late than never
between a rock and a hard place
blow your top
get to the point
like
total, totally
whatever
whole new ball game
you know

Basically, it goes without saying that if we leave no stone unturned and give everyone the benefit of the doubt, you don't have to be a rocket scientist to see that we've got a totally new ball game. Or whatever.

Okay, so you wouldn't pack so many clichés into one sentence. But one is too many.

PREDICTABLE
As poor as a church mouse,
As strong as an ox,
As cute as a button,
As smart as a fox.

As thin as a toothpick,
As white as a ghost,
As fit as a fiddle,
As dumb as a post.

As bald as an eagle,
As neat as a pin,
As proud as a peacock,
As ugly as sin.

As able as an aardvark?

When people are talking,
You know what they'll say
As soon as you hear them
begin a cliché.

From *Lighten Up! 100 Funny Little Poems,* ed. Bruce Lansky. Minnetonka, Minn.: Meadowbrook Press, 1998.

Watch Out for *Very*

Very is a sloppy word. Lazy writers love it! They just add *very* whenever they want to make the meaning of a word more intense; they don't bother to find another word that might be better.

Which of these is stronger?

They were very surprised.

They were astonished.

Breaking the *very* habit may mean that you have to find a new, more expressive word. Or it may just mean that you delete the word *very*. Do it!

Replace ...	with ...
very angry	outraged, furious
very final	final
very necessary	crucial, critical
very stubborn	obstinate, bullheaded
very unique	unique
very weak	frail, feeble, fragile

Use Positive Words

Readers often get a more accurate, livelier picture when you write with positive words.

Negative: He did not arrive on time.
Positive: He arrived late.

Negative: The witness did not speak during the trial.
Positive: The witness was silent during the trial.

Here are some ways to change from negative to positive.

Replace . . .   **with . . .**
did not remember   forgot
was not present   was absent
did not pay attention to   ignored

Search for Synonyms

Our language is rich in synonyms. In other words, we have many ways to say the same thing. Why settle for bland or worn-out words if you have alternatives? It's hard to tell how things differ if they're all "weird" or "cool." Look for more descriptive words: unique, remarkable, bizarre, exotic, grotesque.

If you can't think of a good alternative to a word, look it up in a thesaurus. A thesaurus is not a prehistoric creature, but a kind of dictionary. It suggests different words to use to express a certain concept. A word processor usually has a thesaurus.

Obviously, you should choose the synonym that comes closest to your meaning. Words have different "flavors," different undertones. Take the time to find the right ones. It's crucial when you communicate your ideas.

Look at these examples of snazzy synonyms for plain words.

Word	Alternatives
fast	speedy, swift, rapid, quick, snappy, nimble, agile, breakneck, supersonic
big	huge, gigantic, voluminous, immense, colossal
small	tiny, miniature, petite, pocket-sized
run	dart, charge, dash, gallop, sprint, rush, plunge, scurry, scamper, trot, bolt, scoot
walk slowly	stroll, saunter, dawdle, linger, plod, creep, poke along, trudge

Here's a challenge for you: Think of some other words to practice on—words such as *expensive, smart, think,* or *eat*. How many synonyms can you come up with?

There you have it. Now go out and be a writing powerhouse!

GOOD LUCK!

Glossary

●●●●●●●●●●●●●●●●●●●●●●●●

NOTE: Some entries refer to other words listed in the Glossary. For example, the entry for Active Voice says "See Voice." This means you look under "V" in the Glossary for "Voice" to find the definition of Active Voice. If a page number is listed, turn to that page in this book to find more information about the subject.

Acronym: a word formed from the first letters of a name or title

> GI = **G**overnment **I**ssue
> MVP = **M**ost **V**aluable **P**layer
> radar = **ra**dio **d**etecting **a**nd **r**anging

Active Voice: *See Voice.*

Adjective: a word that modifies (describes, tells more about) a noun or pronoun (*See Parts of Speech.*)

Adverb: a word that modifies (describes, tells more about) a verb, adjective, or other adverb (*See Parts of Speech.*)

Agreement: using the same number (singular or plural) for both subject and verb or for noun and antecedent (*See Number.*)

Analogy: the technique of comparing the similar aspects of things that are otherwise unlike each other (If you compare Earth to a giant spacecraft hurtling through space, you are using an analogy.)

Antecedent: the word, phrase, or clause referred to and replaced by a pronoun (An antecedent precedes, or goes before, the pronoun.)

The word *antecedent* comes from Latin. *Ante* means "before" in Latin; *cedent* comes from the Latin word *cedere,* meaning "to go;" Thus, *ante* + *cedent* = before + to go: to go before.

Antonym: a word with a meaning opposite to that of another word *(See Homonym, Synonym.)*

slow/fast   cool/warm   spicy/bland   hard/soft

Appositive: a noun or noun phrase that explains or identifies the word it immediately follows

Dinah Sawyer, **the school principal,** visited our class.
    appositive

Article: the words *a, an,* and *the (See page 12.)*

Auxiliary Verb: *See Helping Verb.*

Bias: a preference or opinion formed without knowledge or examination of the facts; prejudice *(See page 59.)*

Case: the changes made in nouns or pronouns to show how they are used in a sentence (The English language has three cases: nominative, objective, and possessive.) *(See page 34.)*

✓ *Nominative Case:* a pronoun that is acting as a subject of the sentence

<u>I</u> often enter my stunt kite in contest
subject

✓ *Objective Case:* a pronoun that is the direct or indirect object of a verb or the object of a preposition

The judges awarded **me** first prize.
    indirect object of verb
I will give the kite to **him** tomorrow.
    object of preposition

✓ *Possessive Case:* a pronoun that shows ownership

The kite is **mine.**

Clause: a group of words with a subject and predicate (*See page 41.*)

✓ *Dependent Clause:* a clause that does not express a complete thought (it cannot stand alone as a sentence.)

✓ *Independent Clause:* a clause that expresses a complete thought (It can stand alone as a sentence.)

Cliché: an expression that has lost its originality by being over used ("Between a rock and a hard place" is a cliché.) (*See page 137.*)

Complement: a word that adds to or completes the meaning of a verb (Without the complement, the sentence might not make sense.)

Winning made Quan **happy**.
complement
They elected Maria **president**.
complement

Not all verbs require complements.

Andy **sleeps** late on weekends.
verb

Compound: consisting of two or more words or phrases

✓ *Compound Adjective:* two or more adjectives modifying the same noun (*See page 80.*)

my **prize-winning** kite
compound adjective

✓ *Compound Predicate:* two or more predicates with the same subject (*See page 22.*)

My kite **soared high and stalled**.
compound predicate

✓ *Compound Sentence:* two or more independent clauses *(See page 41.)*

My kite won first prize, but **a gust of wind blew it away**.
independent clause   independent clause

✓ *Compound Subject:* two or more subjects with the same verb or predicate *(See page 22.)*

Kites and hot air balloons are hard to fly in a strong wind.
compound subject

Conjunction: a part of speech that connects words, phrases, and clause *(See Parts of Speech and page 15.)*

✓ *Coordinating Conjunctions* (for example, *and, but, or, nor, for, yet*) connect words, phrases, and clauses of equal importance (independent clauses).

I'd like to fly my kite, **but** I have to do my homework.

✓ *Correlative Conjunctions* are used in pairs: *either . . . or, neither . . . nor, but . . . and, not only . . . but also.*

I like **both** listening to the radio **and** getting A's.

✓ *Subordinating Conjunctions* (for example, *as, as if, because, if, since, unless, when*) connect clauses of unequal importance (an independent and a dependent clause).

I like to listen to the radio **while** I do my homework.

Consonant: all letters other than *a, e, i, o,* and *u (See Vowel.)*

Contraction: a shortened word that is made by replacing some letters with an apostrophe; *can't* for *cannot; I've* for *I have (See page 66–70.)*

Dependent Clause: *See Clause.*

Fragment: a partial sentence that is not a complete thought and lacks a subject or main verb *(See page 46.)*

✓ *Fragment:* Whenever I think I know all the answers.

✓ *Complete:* Whenever I think I know all the answers, life asks a few more questions.

Gerund: a verb form that ends in *-ing* and serves as a noun (*See page 32.*)

> **Winning** is more fun than **losing**.

Helping Verb: a verb used with the main verb to change tense; also called Auxiliary Verb (*See page 25.*)

> My kite **will soar** higher.   My kite **has won** the prize.
> helping main   helping main
> verb   verb   verb   verb

Homonym: words with the same pronunciation but different spelling and meaning; *there, their, they're* (*See Antonym, Synonym, and page 112.*)

Idiom: an expression whose meaning cannot be taken literally, but which is understood by people who live in a certain area or speak a particular language; *hang in there, out of your mind, touch and go*

Independent Clause: *See Clause.*

Infinitive: a verb and its preceding word *to; to sniffle, to cough, to wheeze* (*See page 31.*)

Interjection: an exclamation, such as *Yikes!* or *Cool!* (*See Parts of Speech and page 17.*)

Linking Verb: a verb form of *to be, to seem, to become, to feel,* and *to appear* which connects a subject and something said about the subject; does not take an object (*See page 30.*)

> I **feel** lazy today.
> They **were** absent yesterday.

Lowercase: small letters; opposite of capital letters (*See Uppercase.*)

Metaphor: a comparison made by likening two concepts in order to suggest their similarity (*The dawn of the New Millennium* likens the new millennium to the break of day; *the long arm of the law* gives our system of laws a human body to suggest that the law has similar functions.)

Modifier: a word, phrase, or clause that describes or tells us more about another word, phrase, or clause; should be placed in a sentence in such a way that it's clear which word or words it modifies *(See page 50.)*

> ✓ *Dangling modifiers* have no word in the sentence that they can modify; instead, they "dangle" at the beginning.
>
> > **Dangling:** Walking along the tracks, the train whistled in the distance.
> > **Correct:** Walking along the tracks, I heard the train whistle in the distance.
>
> ✓ *Misplaced modifiers* produce a misleading meaning by being incorrectly placed in a sentence.
>
> > **Misplaced:** You can order gizmos that will be delivered the next day on the Internet.
> > **Correct:** The gizmos you order on the Internet will be delivered to your home the next day.

Nominative Case: *See Case.*

Noun: a part of speech that names things, persons, places, and qualities (*See Parts of Speech and page 8.*)

Number: shows whether a word is singular (one) or plural (two or more) (*See Agreement and page 54.*)

Object: a word that receives the action of a verb; a noun that follows a preposition *(See pages 10,14.)*

   ✓ A *direct object* completes the action of the verb.

   Alyesha **flew** a purple sled **kite**.
         verb   direct object

   ✓ An *indirect object* receives whatever is named by the direct object. It answers the question *To whom?*

   I **gave Alyesha** the purple sled **kite**.
   verb indirect object   direct object

Objective Case: *See Case.*

Paragraph: a group of sentences that develop a common thought or concept *(See page 120.)*

Parallel Construction: using the same grammatical form, such as infinitive or gerund, to state related ideas

   Unparallel: Julia likes swimming, reading, and to skate.
   Parallel: Julia likes swimming, reading, and skating.

Participle: a form of a verb that has two jobs: as an adjective (the *debugging* procedure, *burnt* toast), as a way to show tense (I had *begun;* the film was *shown*) *(See page 33.)*

Parts of Speech: The eight parts of speech are noun, adjective, pronoun, verb, adverb, conjunction, preposition, and interjection. Here's a jingle students used a century or so ago to help them learn about the parts of speech. *See page 8.*

   A NOUN's the name of anything;
   As *school* or *garden, hoop* or *swing.*

   ADJECTIVES tell the kind of noun;
   As *great, small, pretty, white,* or *brown*.

Instead of nouns the PRONOUNS stand:
Their heads, *your* face, *its* paw, *his* hand.

VERBS tell of something being done:
You *read, count, sing, laugh, jump,* or *run.*

How things are done the ADVERBS tell;
As *slowly, quickly, ill,* or *well.*

CONJUNCTIONS join the words together;
As men *and* women, wind *or* weather.

The PREPOSITION stands before
a noun; as, *in* or *through* a door.

The INTERJECTION shows surprise;
As *Oh!* How pretty! *Ah!* How wise!

Passive Voice: *See Voice.*

Person: tells who is the speaker (*first person*), who is spoken to (*second person*), and who is spoken about (*third person*) (*See page 24.*)

Phrase: a group of words that does not make a complete statement

✓ *Prepositional Phrase:* through the window

✓ *Participial Phrase:* soaring through the window

Plural: indicating two or more people or things (*See Agreement.*)

Possessive Case: *See Case.*

Predicate: a word or group of words that makes a statement or asks a question about the subject of a sentence; everything in a sentence that isn't part of the subject (*See page 20.*)

✓ A *simple predicate* is the verb.

✓ A *complete predicate* is the verb plus modifiers, objects, and complements.

✓ A *compound predicate* is two or more verbs with the same subject.

Prefix: a word element like *dis-, un-,* or *ir-* added to the front of the root word to change its meaning: **dis**like, **un**necessary, **ir**regular *(See page 79.)*

Preposition: a part of speech that shows the relationship between a noun and the object of a preposition *(See Parts of Speech and page 14.)*

I entered my **kite in** the **contest**.
noun prep.   object of preposition

Pronoun: a part of speech that takes the place of a noun and is used in order to avoid clumsy repetition *(See Parts of Speech and page 11.)*

Punctuation: the marks that separate writing into phrases, clauses, and sentences to make the meaning clear *(See page 65.)*

Redundant: *adj.,* repetitious; unnecessarily wordy

Root Word: the basic word element to which prefixes and suffixes are added *(See Prefix, Suffix.)*

Run-on: two independent clauses that are separated only by a comma or by no punctuation at all *(See page 48.)*

Sentence: a group of words that has a subject and predicate and that expresses a complete thought

Simile: a comparison of two unlike things using the word *like* or *as*

My new kite is like a dragon with six tails.

Singular: indicating one person or thing *(See Agreement.)*

Spell-checker: word processing software that checks spelling, but can't tell if the wrong word has been used

Subject: what a sentence is about; who or what is doing the action *(See page 20.)*

Suffix: a word element such as *-hood* or *-ity* that is added to the end of a root word and affects its meaning: child**hood**, real**ity** *(See page 93.)*

Synonym: a word similar in meaning to another word *(See Antonym, Homonym.)*

> hazard/danger   movie/film   shout/yell

Tense: the form of a verb that shows time: present, past, future, present perfect, past perfect, future perfect *(See page 25.)*

Topic Sentence: a sentence that presents the main idea of a paragraph; usually begins a paragraph but may appear at the end as a summary statement *(See Page 120.)*

Uppercase: capital letters; opposite of lowercase *(See Lowercase.)*

Verb: a part of speech that describes action, being, or occurrence *(See Parts of Speech and pages 10, 23.)*

Vocabulary: all the words used and understood by an individual

Voice: There are two voices: active and passive. They express the relation between the subject and the action of the verb. In the passive voice, the subject is acted upon. In the active voice, the subject performs the action. *(See page 24.)*

✓ *Passive Voice:* The lawn was mowed by Sylvia.

✓ *Active Voice:* Sylvia mowed the lawn.

Vowel: the letters *a, e, i, o, u,* and sometimes *y* *(See Consonant.)*

Index